SHORT WALKS FROM
——————PUBS IN——————
Kent – the North Downs

David Hancock

COUNTRYSIDE BOOKS
NEWBURY, BERKSHIRE

First published 1996
© David Hancock 1996

COUNTRYSIDE BOOKS
3 Catherine Road
Newbury, Berkshire

ISBN 1 85306 418 1

Designed by Mon Mohan
Cover illustration by Colin Doggett
Photographs by Bonita Toms
Maps by the author

Produced through MRM Associates Ltd., Reading
Printed by Woolnough Bookbinding Ltd., Irthlingborough

Contents

Introduction 5

Walk 1 Knockholt: The Harrow Inn (4½ miles) 7

2 Shoreham: The Crown (3 miles) 12

3 Heaverham: The Chequers Inn (3½ miles) 17

4 Fairseat: The Vigo Inn (2½ miles) 21

5 Thurnham: The Black Horse (3¼ miles) 25

6 Hollingbourne: The Dirty Habit (2 miles) 29

7 Lenham: The Dog and Bear Hotel (2¼ miles) 33

8 Newnham: The George Inn (2½ miles) 37

9 Stalisfield Green: The Plough (4 miles) 42

10 Westwell: The Wheel Inn (4½ miles) 46

11 Hernhill: The Red Lion (2 miles) 51

12 Chilham: The Woolpack Inn (3 miles) 56

13 Wye: The New Flying Horse (4½ miles) 61

14 Bodsham Green: The Timber Batts (3¼ miles) 66

15 Brabourne: The Five Bells (3 miles) 70

16 Pett Bottom: The Duck Inn (3¼ miles) 74

17 ✓ Bridge: The White Horse Inn (3 miles)   79

18 ✓ Chillenden: The Griffin's Head (3½ miles) 84

19 ✓ Alkham: The Marquis of Granby (4 miles) 88

20 ✓ West Hougham: The Chequers (3¼ miles) 93

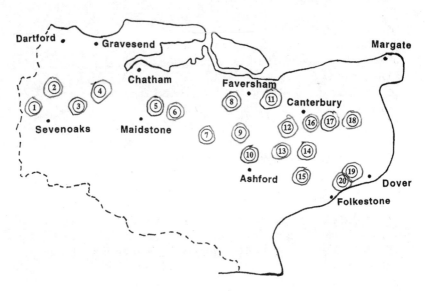

Area map showing the locations of the walks.

Publisher's Note

We hope that you obtain considerable enjoyment from this book; great care has been taken in its preparation. However, changes of landlord and actual closures are sadly not uncommon. Likewise, although at the time of publication all routes followed public rights of way or permitted paths, diversion orders can be made and permissions withdrawn.

We cannot of course be held responsible for such diversion orders and any inaccuracies in the text which result from these or any other changes to the routes, nor any damage which might result from walkers trespassing on private property. We are anxious though, that all details covering the walks and the pubs are kept up to date and would therefore welcome information from readers which would be relevant to future editions.

Introduction

The sweeping chalk escarpment of the North Downs dominates the beautiful Kent countryside – the Garden of England – as it gently arcs across the whole county, from Westerham on the Surrey border to the dramatic white cliffs of Dover. The major attraction of this Area of Outstanding Natural Beauty is the variety of scenery on offer to the visitor, which is best explored and appreciated on foot. Forming a natural barrier between the urban sprawl of London and the rural charm of the Weald, the North Downs comprises a gently dipping backslope hiding peaceful vales and unspoilt villages with typical timbered cottages, medieval manor houses and historic churches, and a lofty chalk ridge that affords magnificent views of the Greensand Hills and the Weald of Kent. Once covered with extensive forest, it is now a rich and varied landscape – a delightful patchwork of rolling, sheep-grazed downland, ancient and coppiced woodland, orchards and hop fields and large tracts of productive farmland – that supports an abundance of wildlife, especially on several designated nature reserves.

The outstanding and absorbing North Downs countryside is probably Kent's major recreational area, attracting an increasing number of walkers, cyclists and car-bound visitors from nearby London and numerous other large towns that exist around its fringe. However, it is for the walking fraternity that the best provision is made. Not only are there established long distance paths – North Downs Way, Pilgrims' Way, Stour Valley Walk, Wealdway, Darent Valley Walk – along its length, or crossing it at some point, but the area is blessed with a superb network of well-waymarked and well-maintained footpaths and bridleways, thanks to the efforts of the County Council. Historically, travellers have used the tracks along the line of the North Downs since Neolithic times, keeping to the drier high ground on their journey from the important centres of Avebury and Stonehenge to Dover. Called the Pilgrims' Way since Victorian times, this route links Canterbury with Winchester, and is popularly associated with Chaucer's *Canterbury Tales* and the journey of pilgrims between the two cathedral cities. Although this was unlikely to have been the case, this romantic tale is kept alive with the names of houses and inns along the route, the latter often linked with a pilgrim story or two.

These 20 short circular walks each radiate out from a friendly country pub and together explore the best of the North Downs countryside, often incorporating sections of the long distance paths. With distances ranging from 2 to 4½ miles they should appeal to family groups and anyone wanting an easy morning or afternoon stroll. All the walks described are along well-waymarked tracks and footpaths, and besides a clear and precise route description there is a detailed sketch map to aid your route finding. However, it is advisable to take the relevant Ordnance Survey 1:50 000 Landranger map with you. If you do find a public right of way obstructed for any reason, please inform the Highways Officer, Highways and Transportation Department, Kent County Council, Springfield, Maidstone, Kent ME14 2LX.

The country pubs and inns featured in this guide have been chosen for their friendly welcome to walkers, the history, character and atmosphere of the building, the quality of food served and their proximity to scenic and interesting walks. Each pub description lists the real ales and other notable drinks and gives a selection of dishes from the menu, indicating whether children and dogs are welcome inside and if there is a garden for summer al fresco drinking. Bar opening and food serving times are also mentioned. Most pubs have a car park and if you are planning to leave your car there while out walking, it is only courteous to ask the landlord's permission first. Alternative parking options are stated, if relevant.

In compiling this selection of walks we would like to thank Derek and Evelyn Hancock for their generous hospitality during our research visits, and for undertaking extra research in Maidstone Reference Library on our behalf. We also acknowledge the co-operation of all the landlords of the pubs included for providing the essential information required.

We hope you gain as much enjoyment out of walking these routes and visiting the pubs involved as we did.

Happy walking!

David Hancock and Bonita Toms
Spring 1996

① Knockholt
The Harrow Inn ✓

Situated on top of the North Downs on the edge of the highest village in Kent, this friendly part-brick and part-weatherboarded inn dates back to the 16th century, the oldest part of the building being the adjoining beamed barn, which now houses the restaurant. Originally the village alehouse, known as the Arrow in 1867, it once possessed a unique signboard, displaying the following rhyme: 'Charles Collins liveth here, sells rum, brandy, gin and beer, I made this board a little wider, to let you know I sell good cyder'. Back in the 1700s, one unwelcome customer was a highwayman who robbed the pub of its takings. After he had fled, so the story goes, some of the customers followed his trail and captured him, promptly bringing him back to the inn and hanging him in the bar. His ghostly presence is said to haunt the pub to this day.

The unassuming single bar is small and homely, featuring a good wintertime open fire, cushioned wall bench seating, rural bygones and a welcoming atmosphere. The adjacent converted barn boasts a wealth of beams and timbers and some interesting prints.

Owned by Shepherd Neame, Britain's oldest brewery, the Harrow serves their full range of real ales on handpump, Best Bitter, Master Brew, Spitfire, Bishops Finger and in winter the rich and full-bodied Original Porter. On the food side, the pub has a sound reputation for its home-made pies – chicken, leek and potato, beef and ale – and, at Sunday lunchtimes, for its choice of three delicious roasts, served with several fresh vegetables. Other items likely to be on the black-board menu are liver and bacon casserole, cottage pie, vegetable moussaka and broccoli and cheese bake, as well as the usual choice of ploughman's lunches and sandwiches. The restaurant is open in the evenings and at Sunday lunchtime, offering, among many other dishes, prawn cocktail, home-made pâté and soup, various steaks and fresh fish. Apple strudel, chocolate cheesecake and nut meringue may appear on the pudding list. Food is served from 11.30 am to 2.30 pm and 6 pm to 11 pm (Sunday 12 noon to 2.30 pm and 7 pm to 10.30 pm).

Well-behaved children are welcome inside, as are dogs. However, on fine summer days families can make use of the rear garden. The Harrow is open from 11 am to 3 pm and 5.30 pm to 11 pm (Sunday 12 noon to 3 pm and 7 pm to 10.30 pm).

Telephone: 01959 532168.

How to get there: Knockholt is located 4½ miles north-west of Sevenoaks and is signposted (1 mile) off the roundabout linking the A224 and B221, adjacent to the M25. From the motorway (junction 5) follow the A25 for Sevenoaks and join the A224 at Riverhead. The pub is easily found on the edge of the village.

Parking: In the pub's own car park opposite. Alternatively, park along Harrow Lane or Chevening Lane, a short distance into the walk.

Length of the walk: 4½ miles. Map: OS Landranger 188 Maidstone and The Weald of Kent (inn GR 596484).

This interesting ramble begins from downland Knockholt, which at 725 ft is the highest village in Kent, then descends the scarp face of the North Downs to the attractive small hamlet of Chevening, with its fine Norman church and magnificent 17th-century mansion (not open). Excellent views of the house are enjoyed from the footpath that traverses its splendid parkland and the steady ascent back to the top of

8

the Downs is rewarded by far-reaching panoramas across the wooded Greensand Ridge, west of Sevenoaks. The circuit is generally well waymarked, using popular woodland, parkland and farmland paths, the latter part following the North Downs Way.

The Walk

1 On leaving the pub turn left along Harrow Road towards the village centre. Just before reaching a road junction and the Three Horsehoes pub, turn left into Chevening Lane, a narrow dead-end lane leading to the top of the North Downs. Pass several cottages, then where the tarmac ends at a gate (private property) bear left with the North Downs Way sign and immediately right beside a stile to follow the right-hand edge of a field. Shortly, head steeply downhill on a narrow hedged path, pausing to savour the occasional cameo views through the foliage, eventually reaching a stile. Descend along the right-hand side of two pasture fields with delightful views across Chevening Park and back along the wooded scarp face of the North Downs.

2 At the base of the Downs, keep ahead along the straight path, disregarding the arrowed stile on your right into Chevening Park, and continue for a ¼ mile to enter St Botoloph's churchyard and the hamlet of Chevening – well worth further exploration. 'Kent has no lovelier corner so near to London' was how Arthur Mee described Chevening, a charming settlement dominated by its great house and parkland. Dating from 1625 and designed by Inigo Jones, Chevening House was the home of the Stanhope family before becoming the official residence of the Foreign Secretary in 1957, a good enough reason for it not being open to the public. The mainly Norman church houses some fine tombs and memorials and is dedicated to a patron saint of travellers. The Pilgrims' Way once passed through the Park, and pilgrims travelling from Winchester to Canterbury would have reached here on the seventh day of their journey. The eccentric 3rd Earl Stanhope closed this section of the route in 1792.

Retrace your steps back along the narrow path towards the Downs and climb the stile passed earlier into Chevening Park. Keep left-handed along the fence and enjoy the fine views of the mansion away to your left. Cross a metalled drive close to a cattle-grid, then follow the fence right-handed, gently climbing to a stile and a track. Bear left, then in a few yards where the track curves sharp left, bear off right through a metal kissing-gate. Begin ascending steeply along the edge of a field, negotiate a walk-through stile and proceed through a copse

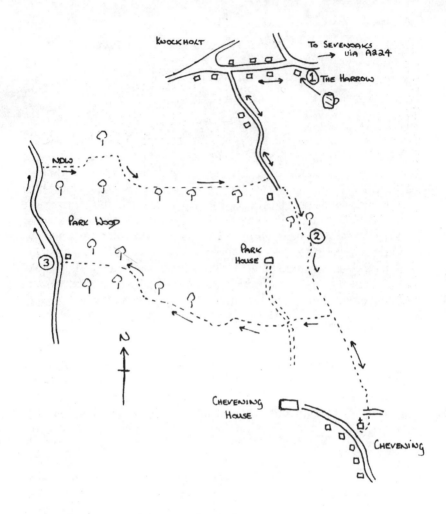

to a stile. Maintain direction, uphill to a further stile and pause to catch your breath and to savour the magnificent views. Gradually climb through woodland on a wide path, which soon bears left, eventually reaching a lane by Keepers Cottage.

3 Turn right along the lane, soon pass a North Downs Way fingerpost on your left, then, at a crossing of paths, follow the waymarked North Downs Way right over a stile and along the edge of woodland. This well signposted section passes through a copse to a stile, then along the edge of a large field to reach a small fenced off area accessed via a gate. This has been specifically created for walkers

Chevening church.

to enter and observe a special view off the North Downs. Through a niche cut out of the trees you will see Chevening House perfectly framed at the base of the hill. Continue on the well-worn path to reach Chevening Lane, turning left to retrace your outward steps back into Knockholt and the Harrow Inn.

Places of interest nearby

South of the M25 among the wooded slopes of the Greensand Ridge are the National Trust properties of *Chartwell* and *Emmetts Garden*. *Chartwell* is the former home of Sir Winston Churchill and is filled with reminders of the great statesman, including paintings, uniforms and gifts presented to him. Delightful gardens and far-reaching views. Telephone: 01732 866368. *Emmetts Garden* is a charming hillside shrub garden, with bluebells in spring and fine autumn colours. Telephone: 01732 750367 and 750429. Nearby Sevenoaks is dominated by *Knole House and Park* (National Trust), with the largest private house in England, which dates from 1456 and contains important collections of furniture and paintings in 13 sumptuously decorated state rooms. Magnificent deer park. Telephone: 01732 450608.

Shoreham ✓
The Crown

The appealing village of Shoreham straddles the meandering river Darent and boasts some fine Georgian houses, numerous old cottages, a splendid 15th-century church and, surprisingly, five pubs. The friendly Crown, built in 1454, is one of the three oldest buildings in the village and was originally a lot smaller and thatched, the wattle and daub and thatch being replaced by brick and tiles in 1666. Records state that the first five innkeepers were also farmers, with the land around the pub being farmed up until the late 19th century. It is also associated with a fascinating tale in the village. In the early 1800s smugglers arrived at the inn with with a wounded Spaniard, who was nursed back to health by the landlord's daughter. Once fully recovered he married the daughter but was later press-ganged into the Navy, leaving his wife expecting their child. He returned many years later to learn that she had died while giving birth and promptly took his own life. It is said that the Spaniard haunts the pub, his footsteps having been heard on several occasions.

The interior comprises three unpretentious bars, including a small simply adorned public bar and a comfortable beamed lounge furnished with darkwood tables and chairs. A cosy adjacent bar, reached via a couple of steps, features a large inglenook fireplace with warming log fires in winter. Those of you who have foraged for chestnuts during the walk are welcome to make use of the roasting pan by the fire.

The pub is owned by Greene King and dispenses their IPA and Abbot real ales, as well as a brewery seasonal ale, such as Black Baron. It is a popular destination with walkers at lunchtime for the good value bar food on offer. The short printed menu offers standard pub favourites like a range of basket meals, cottage pie, ham, egg and chips and fish, chips and peas. Hearty snacks include a home-made soup, French bread filled with either sausage, beef or cheese, or excellent freshly-cut sandwiches, perhaps filled with home-cooked ham. Hot daily specials may include chicken tikka masala, ham and cheese crêpes, beef curry or steak and kidney pie. Food is served daily, except Sunday evenings, from 12 noon to 2 pm and 7 pm to 9.30 pm.

The sheltered rear garden has various white plastic tables and chairs, weathered pews under a clear perspex roof and is the setting for regular summer barbecues. Dogs are welcome in the bars, but children are not allowed inside. The Crown is open from 11.30 am to 3 pm and 7 pm to 11 pm (Sunday 12 noon to 3 pm and 7 pm to 10.30 pm).

Telephone: 01959 522903.

How to get there: Shoreham is located in the Darent valley, ½ mile off the A225 between Sevenoaks and Dartford, 4½ miles north of Sevenoaks. From the M25 (junction 5), follow the A25 east through Riverhead to pick up the north-bound A225 in a mile. The Crown is situated at the northern end of the High Street on the edge of the village.

Parking: There is a small car park at the pub. If it is full, park along the street south of the pub, or use the free village car park at the southern end of the High Street.

Length of the walk: 3 miles. Map: OS Landranger 188 Maidstone and The Weald of Kent (inn GR 518620).

This delightful circuit explores the attractive Darent valley and the charming old village of Shoreham, which, unbelievably, lie within 5 miles of Orpington and the end of the outward sprawl of London. As a result, both village and valley are popular with visitors and walkers, especially at weekends. Waymarked paths traverse the wooded valley side, affording excellent views over the village, and the return route crosses a golf course and follows the river back into Shoreham, which is well worth closer inspection.

The Walk

1 From the pub turn right along the road and soon leave the village confines. When the footway ends, remain on the road – taking great care for it can be busy – as it ascends out of the valley. Within 250 yards, beyond a house called Little Field, take the arrowed footpath left and climb the short distance to reach a further metalled lane. Turn sharp left (waymarker post) just before the lane and follow a track, which soon bears right to a barrier. Walk beside the barrier and gently climb to a fork of paths on the edge of Meenfield Wood (sign).

Keep left, pass beside a further barrier and follow the yellow arrowed route along a delightful path, affording cameo views across Shoreham and the Darent valley. Well-placed benches tempt you to linger awhile to absorb the peaceful scene. In approximately ½ mile, disregard the arrowed path left which leads back down to Shoreham, unless you only desire a short stroll and more time to amble around the village.

2 Continue along this excellent level path which traverses the valley side above the village and passes through the edge of Meenfield Wood, eventually reaching a stile on the woodland fringe. Before turning left downhill through pasture along a line of mature beech trees, bear right and pause for a few minutes on the splendidly positioned bench that makes the most of the far-reaching views across Sevenoaks and the wooded Greensand Ridge. At the end of the beech trees, climb a stile flanking a gate and gently descend a good track to reach a lane. Cross straight over to follow a metalled lane (no through road) leading to Kennel Cottage, a fine timbered building which boasts a 'Historic Building of Kent' plaque.

3 Where the tarmac ends continue along a bridleway beside a stream and shortly cross a footbridge beside an old ford. Join a good track, soon cross the river Darent and pass the entrance to Home Farm. The farm is a converted watermill, one of two former mills in

14

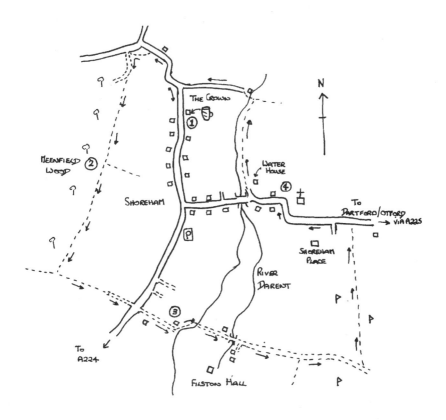

the village, and once milled corn as far back as 1086. Nearby is Filston Hall, a Tudor manor house restyled in the 17th century and regarded as an outstanding example of a small country manor house. It still stands on its original moat fed from the Darent and was once the home of the Colegate family, a name famous around the world for toothpaste. The track becomes metalled and ascends beside a golf course. Look out for a waymarked path left which cuts across a cricket pitch and between the fairways and tees of the golf course to reach a lane, close to the modern clubhouse. Turn left downhill in the village, passing the entrance to Shoreham Place on your left.

4 Opposite the Old George Inn you will find the beautiful church of St Peter and St Paul, with an avenue of neatly trimmed yews leading to its fine porch, which is formed from the root of a huge upended oak tree that once grew in the churchyard. It dates from the 15th century and has a well proportioned 18th-century red-brick tower, one of the best examples of a medieval carved rood screen in England and an organ that was originally erected in Westminster Abbey in 1730.

Having visited the church, proceed along the village street to reach the bridge over the river Darent. Venture across the bridge to the Kings Arms, to view what may be the last surviving ostler's box, a kind of horseman's cubby-hole, where the ostler would wait to look after the customers' horses. Otherwise, bear right along the waymarked Darent Valley Walk before the bridge and shortly pass the gates to Water House. This was home to Samuel Palmer, the visionary painter, from 1827 to 1834. He used the village as a background in his strange and touching pastoral paintings, and the great poet and artist William Blake was a regular visitor.

Follow the charming path alongside the river, then just beyond some cottages on the opposite bank, cross a footbridge into Mill Lane. The former corn mill, which was later adapted to make paper between 1690 and 1926, can be seen on your right. Walk up this attractive lane to a T-junction and turn left along the High Street back to the Crown.

Places of interest nearby

A few miles north of Shoreham is *Lullingstone Park*, originally a medieval deer park, now managed for recreation and conservation. There is a visitor centre. Telephone: 01322 865995. A riverside walk will lead to historic *Lullingstone Castle*, favoured by Henry VII and Queen Anne. Telephone: 01322 862114. Close by is *Lullingstone Roman Villa* which dates from the first century AD and displays well-preserved mosaic floors. Telephone: 01322 863467.

Heaverham ✓
The Chequers Inn

This neatly maintained red-brick and ragstone built inn nestles beside a peaceful country lane in the centre of a tiny estate village at the base of the North Downs. Little is known about the early history of the building, except that it dates from the 17th century and was originally constructed as an alehouse for the estate workers. Until recently it was owned by the estate of St Clere, an imposing 17th-century mansion, and the village was once a thriving farming community with the former cowsheds and dairy being located opposite the inn.

Inside, there is an unspoilt and old-fashioned public bar with lino flooring – ideal for walkers – scrubbed tables, rustic chairs and cushioned benches, a small brick fireplace and an attractive collection of hunting and racing prints decorating the walls. The carpeted lounge bar with an open log fire in winter offers more comfort for diners, while the original 17th-century Kentish barn adjacent to the inn houses the cosy restaurant, complete with heavy oak beams.

The Chequers is a Shepherd Neame house, offering their well-kept Master Brew, Spitfire and Bishops Finger on handpump for the real ale enthusiast. Hungry walkers with a hearty appetite will not be disappointed with the varied and extensive lunchtime menu. Freshly-baked bread accompanies ploughman's lunches and home-made soup, and makes the generously filled sandwiches. Main meals range from steak and kidney pudding and cod and chips to Thai curry and bubble and squeak with ham and eggs. The imaginative evening menu follows a Shakespearian theme with courses, or 'acts', named after plays. Regular choices include dressed crab, lamb goulash, game pie and Cajun chicken, supplemented by weekly changing specials, such as bison with Guinness and woodland mushrooms, moules masala and occasionally kangaroo! Traditional Sunday lunch is a popular feature. There is also a wide selection of vegetarian dishes and children have their own menu. Food is served from 12 noon to 2.30 pm and 7 pm to 9.30 pm (10 pm Friday and Saturday, 9 pm Sunday). Food is not available on Monday evenings in winter.

Both children and dogs are most welcome indoors and there is even a jar of dog biscuits on the bar for hungry canine customers. Sunny summer days can be enjoyed in the lovely lawned garden with picnic benches, mature trees and relaxing rural views. The Chequers is open from 11 am to 3 pm and 6 pm to 11 pm (Sunday 12 noon to 3 pm and 7 pm to 10.30 pm). In winter months the pub may be closed all day every other Monday.

Telephone: 01732 761413.

How to get there: Heaverham lies a mile east of Kemsing and 4 miles north-east of Sevenoaks. It is easily accessible from the A225 at Otford, the M26 (junction 2A), the A20 and the A227 via Wrotham and the A25 at Seal, near Sevenoaks, via Kemsing station. The Chequers is situated in the centre of the small hamlet.

Parking: There is adequate parking at the inn.

Length of the walk: 3½ miles. Map: OS Landranger 188 Maidstone and The Weald of Kent (inn GR 572587).

After strolling through the pretty hamlet of Heaverham, this scenic ramble traverses the St Clere Estate before steeply ascending the scarp face of the Downs on the well-waymarked North Downs Way. Good estate, farmland and woodland paths, and the magnificent vistas from the top, make the climb well worth the effort.

18

The Walk

1 Turn right on leaving the pub and follow the quiet lane through the charming hamlet. Shortly, turn right again in front of a converted oast house, signposted 'Wrotham'. Where this lane curves sharp left, keep ahead along a waymarked path which follows the metalled drive through the St Clere Estate. The fine coral red-brick mansion, built in 1633 for the Parliamentarian Sir John Sedley, soon comes into view on your left with the tree-clad North Downs as its backdrop. One owner considered the house to have 'the fairest view in Kent', but the rather close presence of the M26 may well have spoilt its peaceful outlook.

Remain on the tarmac drive to reach a lane beyond East Lodge, in a collection of dwellings and farms known as Yaldham. Turn left along the lane for 400 yards to a sharp left-hand bend at the base of the North Downs.

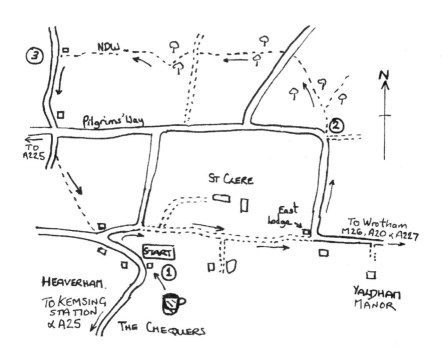

2   Enter the field directly ahead (yellow arrow) to join the North Downs Way. Follow the defined path, gradually ascending across a field to a stile, then continue steeply uphill to a further stile on the edge of woodland. Pause for a moment to catch your breath and take in the stunning view that has unfolded, across the wooded Greensand Ridge near Ightham. At a fork of paths beyond the stile, proceed straight on with North Downs Way sign, climbing wooden steps to a lane. Briefly turn right, then follow the fingerpost left and gently climb on a good path through woodland, eventually reaching a gate on the edge of the trees. Continue along the left-hand edge of a field beside woodland, soon to pick up an open earth track along the top of the Downs, affording breathtaking views south, east and west.

Go straight over a crossing of tracks, climb a stile on the edge of woodland and keep to the North Downs Way through the trees to a stile. Turn right along the edge of the field beyond, cross a further stile and maintain direction towards a building. Shortly, cross a stile, then follow a line of posts to join a defined track leading towards a corrugated roofed barn and negotiate a stile flanking a gate onto a lane.

3   Turn left along Cotman's Ash Lane and steadily descend off the North Downs. Beyond a house called Pilgrims – so called as it lies adjacent to the ancient Pilgrims' Way linking Winchester and Canterbury – go over a crossroads, and in a few yards take the arrowed path on your left. Bear diagonally right across a field on a worn path towards an oast house, shortly reaching the lane in Heaverham. Turn left back through the hamlet for the Chequers Inn.

Places of interest nearby

Dominating the attractive town of Sevenoaks and 4½ miles south-west of Heaverham, is *Knole House and Park* (National Trust) with the largest private house in England, set in a magnificent deer park owned by Lord Sackville. Telephone: 01732 450608. Ancient *Otford* (3 miles west) has the ruins of a palace in which Becket once lived, and the church at *Wrotham* (3 miles east) dates from the 13th century and boasts an unusual tower and one of the oldest church clocks (17th century) in the country. Near Wrotham Heath (2 miles further south-east) is *Nepicar Farm,* a working farm with rare breeds, farm walks, children's play area, cheese-making, granary displays and tearoom. Telephone: 01732 883040.

Fairseat ✓
The Vigo Inn

Located on the crest of the North Downs, this extremely old pub dates back to 1471 and the time of the cattle drovers, when it was called the Upper Drover Inn – the Lower Drover Inn being positioned at the base of the hill. It acquired its present name after the battle of Vigo Bay in 1702, where the English were victorious over a Spanish treasure fleet. During the battle, a Fairseat man saved the life of Admiral Sir George Rooke, the Fleet Commander, who showed his gratitude on his return by purchasing the inn for his rescuer and hence the name was changed to commemorate the event. During the coaching era it became a posting house on the busy Tonbridge to Gravesend turnpike. It was renovated and modernised in 1950, during which a cubby-hole was uncovered. This was probably used to hide young lads from the press gangs, as well as concealing smugglers and their contraband.

The Vigo remains a classic, unspoilt alehouse with two simply adorned, yet very neat and tidy bars. Each is warmed by a wood-burning stove, the larger bar featuring a fine inglenook fireplace, a red and black tiled floor, lovely old darkwood pub furniture and a couple of heavy beams. Pride of place in the small bar goes to the only remaining Dadlums table in the county – a Kentish form of table skittles. Despite having few frills, the inn offers a warm welcome and a traditional atmosphere where conversation rules, not piped music.

Lovers of real ale will not be disappointed at this freehouse, for it's a real drinkers' haunt, dispensing Harveys Sussex Bitter, Young's Bitter and five frequently changing guest brews, such as Goacher's Mild, Young's Special, Harveys Porter, Jolly Roger Flagship and Kilkenny Irish Beer. Also available on draught are Addlestones cider, Guinness and an interesting range of lagers. As one would expect from this staunchly traditional pub, food is limited to a selection of freshly-made sandwiches and rolls, accompanied by pickled onions or pickled eggs.

Dogs on leads and families with young children are very welcome indoors, as there is no outside seating. Unusual events to note are the pickled onion tasting and conker contests, a search for the best specimens. The pub is open from 12 noon to 2.30 pm and 6 pm to 11 pm (Sunday 12 noon to 3 pm and 7 pm to 10.30 pm).

Telephone: 01732 822547.

How to get there: The Vigo Inn is located on top of the North Downs beside the A227 Tonbridge to Gravesend road, 8½ miles south of Gravesend and 1½ miles north of the A20 and M20 (junction 2) at Wrotham.

Parking: There are a few spaces in front of the inn and a car park across the adjacent lane.

Length of the walk: 2½ miles. Map: OS Landranger 188 Maidstone and the Weald of Kent (inn GR 631610).

This is a delightful short walk incorporating the North Downs Way, the ancient Pilgrims' Way and the beautiful 160 acre Trosley Country Park, with its network of scenic downland and woodland paths, rich plant and animal life and spectacular views over the deep patchwork of the Weald of Kent. The circuit is well waymarked and involves a steady descent and steep ascent of the scarp face of the North Downs.

The Walk

1 On leaving the inn, turn left along the footway beside the busy A227 for a short distance, soon to bear off left onto the North Downs Way (waymarker). Follow a good wide track, pass a lodge and an old gateway, keeping ahead alongside a walled garden, and steadily descend a stony and flinty route, which affords excellent views along the wooded scarp face of the Downs.

Near the base of the hill, turn left at a T-junction of byways to follow the Pilgrims' Way, here a defined wide path that skirts the base of the North Downs with views across rolling countryside. Just beyond a thatched cottage, turn right along a lane at the bottom of Vigo Hill and pass Pilgrims' House. At a sharp right-hand bend, bear off left along a peaceful metalled stretch of the Pilgrims' Way.

2 Pass a number of dwellings on your right and a waymarked footpath leading to the charming old village of Trottiscliffe with its tiny green, attractive cottages and fascinating church. A few steps beyond this path, bear off left with a footpath fingerpost and pass beside a five-bar gate to enter Trosley Country Park. Covering some 160 acres of the woodland and chalk downland, the country park was once part of the extensive Waterlow Estate, in which was sited a mansion called Trosley Towers. No longer in existence, it was once owned by Sir Sydney Hedley Waterlow, one of the founders of the great Waterlow printing firm.

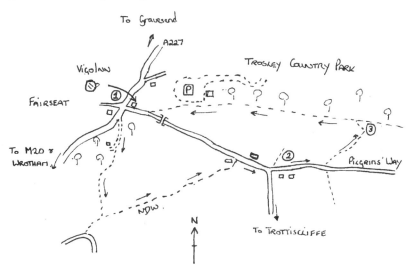

Cross a stile by a further gate and head diagonally right on a clear path to reach a waymarker post. Continue straight ahead (Blue Walk 4) and ascend steeply at an angle up the chalk face of the North Downs. On reaching a wooden gate, rest awhile to absorb the superb view across the Weald.

3 Beyond the gate, follow the Blue Walk marker left, climbing a series of steps to join one of the main paths through this beautiful park. It consists of mixed woodland – beech, oak, ash and yew – and expanses of chalk grassland, which are rich in herbs, flowers and insects, particularly butterflies. Eight types of orchid are known to grow here, as well as rock roses and cowslips. The information centre has various leaflets, including nature trail guides to the colour coded short walks.

Unless you wish to explore the network of paths in the country park, turn left along the main path and follow this level route through rich woodland and scrub along the ridge of the North Downs. An unusual throne-like seat, carved from the trunk of a fallen tree, provides a splendid spot for a rest and to enjoy the cameo view across the Weald. Continue past the picnic area, toilets, information centre and refreshment kiosk to reach a road – the top of Vigo Hill. Turn right for the short stroll back to the main road and the Vigo Inn.

Places of interest nearby

Trosley Country Park is open daily all year from 9 am to dusk with the visitor centre opening at peak times. Telephone: 01732 823570. A mile east of Trottiscliffe is the *Coldrum Long Barrow* (National Trust), a megalithic burial chamber surrounded by standing stones. The tomb was opened in 1910 and 22 skeletons were found, dating from 3,000 BC. In Meopham (3 miles north) is *Meopham Windmill*, an unusual six-sided smock mill, built in 1801 and overlooking the attractive village green. It contains the original machinery and is in working order since being restored in 1927. Open on Sundays and bank holidays in summer. Telephone: 01474 812110. Just south of Wrotham Heath (3½ miles south) is *Great Comp Garden,* a fine 7 acre garden with a wide variety of trees, shrubs, heathers and herbaceous plants, as well as terraces, formal and woodland walks. Telephone: 01732 882669.

5 Thurnham
The Black Horse

Tucked beneath the steep face of the North Downs on the Pilgrims' Way and named after an influential Norman family, diminutive Thurnham is a peaceful, off-the-beaten-track village. Despite its size, it possesses the remains of a Norman castle, a well-maintained church founded in the 12th century and a splendid half-timbered and herringbone brick house called The Friars, in the grounds of which an Anglo-Saxon burial ground was discovered in 1913.

Almost opposite is the Black Horse, a homely and welcoming pub that makes the most of its lofty position, with an attractive lawned garden and paved patio enjoying views across Maidstone and the Medway valley – ideal for summer al fresco imbibing. The actual age of the premises is not known, but in the early 18th century it may well have been a forge with adjoining barns and stables and owned by the Fuller family. Between 1744 and 1751 the buildings were converted into a pub and given the present name. A severe fire in 1988 seriously damaged the old structure, resulting in significant rebuilding and modernisation, including a new extension.

The comfortable open-plan bar with adjacent dining area features a brick fireplace with gas 'log-effect' fire, red plush covered stools, chairs and benches, darkwood tables and chairs and a collection of bank notes above and behind the bar.

Owned by Whitbread, the Black Horse serves a varied range of real ales, such as Fremlins Bitter, Boddingtons and changing guest ales like Wadworth 6X, Tetley Bitter and Fuller's London Pride. There is also a good selection of lagers, stouts and bottled beers. Intending diners can choose a dish or two from the large blackboard menu in the bar, which generally lists various sandwiches, filled hot baps and ploughman's lunches, as well as regular items like garlic mushrooms, prawn cocktail, home-made burgers, ham, egg and chips, mixed grill and chicken Kiev. Daily specials may include barbecue pork kebabs, cottage pie, liver and onions and Italian pasta dishes – basil and tomato or olive and tomato. Food is served on Tuesday to Saturday from 12 noon to 2 pm and 7 pm to 9 pm.

Children and dogs are welcome inside and in the pretty garden, which is complete with flower borders, shrubs and picnic benches. The Monday quiz night in winter is a popular attraction. The pub is open from 11 am (12 noon in winter) to 2.30 pm and 6 pm to 11 pm (Sunday 12 noon to 3 pm and 7 pm to 10.30 pm).

Telephone: 01622 737185.

How to get there: Thurnham is situated 1 mile east of the A249 Maidstone to Sittingbourne road, via Detling, and 3½ miles north-east of Maidstone. The Black Horse can be found on the Pilgrims' Way at the crossroads in the centre of the hamlet.

Parking: The pub has a large car park adjacent.

Length of the walk: 3¼ miles. Map: OS Landranger 188 Maidstone and the Weald of Kent (inn GR 807579).

Having crossed the level lower slopes of the North Downs on good farmland and paddock paths, this scenic and often challenging circuit ascends an ancient track to join the North Downs Way, which dips and climbs along the crest of the scarp slope. The route can be muddy, but there are magnificent views and the chance to explore some fascinating historic sites.

26

The Walk

1 From the pub and crossroads turn right downhill and soon take the arrowed bridleway left, opposite the postbox in the wall. You could, however, continue a few yards further along the lane to visit the church of St Mary the Virgin, neatly tucked away down a leafy path. Dating from Norman times, it features a 14th-century tower, memorials to several local familes and, in the beautifully maintained churchyard, the grave of Alfred Mynn (1807-61), the famous Victorian Kent cricketer.

The bridleway (blue arrows) follows a long metalled drive to Thurnham Keep Farm, a converted oast house, then where the tarmac ends, you keep ahead along a worn path to a gate. Pass in front of Aldington Court Cottages and cross the stile ahead, as the drive curves sharp left. Proceed along a defined straight track between broad fields to reach a lane near Cobham Manor Oast, one of the first in Kent to be converted into a house.

2 Turn left, then almost immediately right (waymarked) into the riding stables complex. Keep right, following the yellow arrow between the tack room and stables, then alongside the coffee shop and between outdoor exercise areas, at the end of which you turn right. Shortly, bear left up concrete steps to a stile and enter a paddock. Keep to the right-hand edge to a further stile beyond a gateway and maintain direction through another paddock with numerous horse jumps. Climb a stile, cross a grassy scrub area, then beyond a further stile join a narrow, fenced path alongside a hedge.

On nearing a house (Whitehall), follow the arrowed diversion right around the garden to a track. Turn left and ascend the metalled drive to reach the Pilgrims' Way. This ancient route has been used by people since Neolithic times, some 5,000 years ago, and more recently as a path for pilgrims travelling to the shrine of St Thomas Becket at Canterbury. Bear slightly left and cross the lane onto an arrowed byway that ascends steadily towards the scarp face of the Downs. This track is called Coldharbour Lane and probably as far back as Roman times, there was a building or ruin along its route in which travellers could shelter, or 'camp out' for the night, hence the unusual name.

3 On reaching an arrowed post turn left to join the North Downs Way and steeply climb on a worn path beside yew hedges to the top of Cat's Mount and the crest of the North Downs. Occasional breaks in the trees afford some of the finest views to be had from the North Downs Way. Shortly, descend sharply through trees to a stile beside a

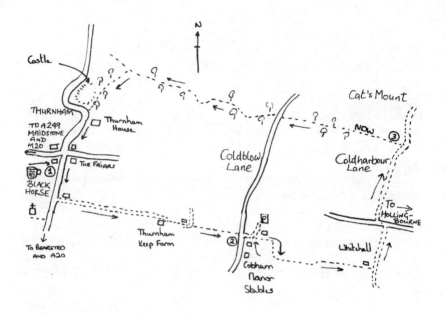

gate and cross a narrow metalled lane (Coldblow Lane). Remain on the Way as it climbs past a barrier, becoming a delightful wooded path. This fairly level route is short lived, as the Way soon dips and climbs through yew and beech woods via a series of energy-sapping wooden steps, which can be slippery in wet weather.

The roller-coaster route gives way to a gentle ascent along the left-hand edge of an open field, rewarding your efforts with panoramic views across the Medway valley. Eventually, reach a waymarker post at the head of a combe and follow the North Downs Way arrow left. Walk along a defined path at the base of scrub, your route soon levelling out as you pass behind Thurnham House to reach a lane halfway up Thurnham Hill.

Hidden in the trees and scrubland up to your right is the remains of Thurnham or Goddard's Castle, a motte-and-bailey style castle built in the late 11th or early 12th century. To explore the site, it is best to turn right at the lane, following it uphill to pick up a path on your right leading to this one time Norman stronghold of the 'de Thurnham' family. The main route heads left, steeply downhill on meeting the lane, soon to reach the village crossroads with the Pilgrims' Way and the Black Horse.

28

6 Hollingbourne ✓
The Dirty Habit ✓

As its new name, its original name – the Pilgrims Rest – and the inn's position beside the Pilgrims' Way suggest, this fine hostelry could have been an important destination for weary travellers undertaking the long trek from Winchester to Canterbury cathedral, to see Thomas Becket's shrine between the late 13th and 14th centuries. A building stood on this site during the reign of William the Conqueror (1066-87), but this is believed to have been destroyed by an earthquake in 1382. During Chaucer's time (1340-1400) and the writing of the *Canterbury Tales,* the new building was a farmhouse with adjoining cottages and was occupied by monks who introduced wine and ale to the premises. They would have offered accommodation and sustenance to the tired and hungry pilgrims on their way to Canterbury. In 1666 the Pilgrims Rest was acquired by a London merchant – Samuel Aellard – who replaced the thatch, wattle and daub with fashionable clay tiles and brickwork. During the 18th century a Georgian façade was added and the premises were called the King's Head to honour the reigning monarch. That name remained unchanged until 1975 when it reverted to the Pilgrims Rest, and in 1992 the pub was given its present name, reflecting the humour and character portrayed in Chaucer's story.

The cosy interior is full of atmosphere, with beams, panelled walls, some exposed brick, a rustic collection of old pine pews and stripped tables and an enormous inglenook fireplace with flame-effect gas fire on cold days. The ambience is enhanced by dim lighting, candlelit tables and an extra open log fire in winter. It is a lively place with good piped music and live blues music every Monday evening and Sunday lunchtime.

A well-stocked bar dispenses up to six real ales, such as Bass, Boddingtons and Younger No 3, Scrumpy Jack cider, four draught lagers, a range of malt whiskies and a short, interesting list of wines. The bar food is imaginative, home-cooked and of good quality. Light snacks include filled baguettes, ploughman's lunches, avocado crab gratin and warm salad of pan-fried pigeon breast. Regular main course options feature lasagne, stir-fried chicken, pasta with pesto sauce and shredded beef with black bean sauce, with the daily specials board listing items like mussels in wine and garlic, medallions of monkfish on a prawn sauce and pan-fried Scotch rump steak. Desserts include American apple pie and tiramisu. Food is served daily from 12 noon to 2 pm and 7 pm to 9 pm.

Dogs are welcome inside, but children are not really catered for or encouraged. However, they are allowed in the attractive and sheltered rear patio with tables and chairs and tubs of flowers. The pub is open from 11.30 am to 3 pm and 6.30 pm to 11 pm (Sunday 12 noon to 3 pm and 7 pm to 10.30 pm).

Telephone: 01622 880210.

How to get there: Hollingbourne is located on the B2163 south of Sittingbourne, 1½ miles north of the A20 and M20 (junction 8), 4 ½ miles east of Maidstone. The Dirty Habit is situated in the upper village, just north of the church and on the lower slope of the North Downs.

Parking: The pub has a good car park to the rear.

Length of the walk: 2 miles. Map: OS Landranger 188 Maidstone and The Weald of Kent (inn GR 845554).

This delightful short ramble follows the North Downs Way as it ascends from the village across farmland and open grassland to the crest of the North Downs – the perfect spot to rest, watch the paragliders and absorb the panoramic views across the Weald. After a short stretch of woodland, the route descends an old byway before returning to Hollingbourne on a level bridleway. Make time to visit the historic church.

The Walk

1   On leaving the pub cross the B2163 and turn right along this busy road to pass the road (Pilgrims' Way) to Thurnham. Shortly, take the waymarked path on your left (North Downs Way), which ascends through trees above the road to reach an open field. Proceed along the right-hand edge of this field, gradually climbing on a worn path towards the steep scarp slope of the Downs. Go through a swing gate flanking double wooden gates and why not pause here, either to take in the splendid country views that have unfolded behind you, or to prepare yourself for the strength-sapping climb ahead of you.

Bear half-left through scrub, then ascend very steeply up the grassy scarp slope on a defined path, keeping left on reaching dense scrubland. The excellent path continues to climb steadily, but frequent stops, to catch your breath and to admire the far-reaching views across Hollingbourne to Leeds Castle and beyond to the wooded Greensand Ridge, make the effort seem well worthwhile.

2   Leave the grassy downland via a wooden swing gate and follow a wide, fenced path, cutting through a copse along the crest of the Downs. Beyond a further swing gate, keep to the North Downs Way across grassy commonland, soon to go through a further gate into woodland. Proceed along a narrow, meandering path through the splendid mixed woodland to reach a red waymarked post and a junction of routes. Turn left and begin your descent off the Downs on an ancient byway, disregarding the North Downs Way off to your right. At the base of this yew-fringed old lane pass Allington Farm and follow its drive to a narrow metalled lane (Pilgrims' Way).

3   Turn left and ignore the first path arrowed right, then shortly take the waymarked bridleway right, just before Little Allington. Follow the good track between broad fields, bear sharp left with the track by a pumping station and head towards an oast house. Pass Penn Oast and keep to the metalled drive to reach the B2163 beside Hollingbourne Court, a fine example of an Elizabethan manor house with

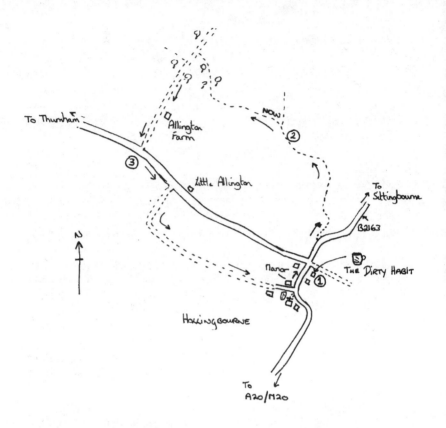

impressive Tudor chimneys, elaborate brickwork and lofty gables. It was once the home of the ubiquitous Culpeper family, who crop up all over Kent, including owning Leeds Castle. The manor overlooks the fine 14th-century church of All Saints which houses the Culpeper chapel, specially built in the 17th century to contain the white marble tomb of Lady Elizabeth Culpeper who died in 1638. Among the other treasures in the church is the famous Culpeper needlework, a richly decorated altar cloth that was embroidered in gold thread by four Culpeper daughters over 300 years ago. It took twelve years to complete and features fruits of all kinds, including Kentish hops and the hazelnut, but when not in use, it is kept locked away. However, it may be seen on application to the vicar.

Having visited the church and its lovely environs, follow the road uphill, passing a number of fine dwellings, notably the magnificent half-timbered Malthouse, and shortly reach the Dirty Habit.

Lenham ✓
The Dog and Bear Hotel

The village square at Lenham must be one of the prettiest in Kent, with its fine mixture of Georgian houses and medieval timber-framed dwellings, notably the magnificent 15th-century timbered hall house on the corner of Headcorn Road, now housing the pharmacy. In 1946, during extensive restoration work, the skeletons of three 6th-century men were found alongside a small collection of Saxon weapons here.

Pride of place in the square, however, goes to the attractive, long, cream-painted Dog and Bear Hotel, which was built in 1602 as a coaching inn to serve weary travellers using the London to Folkestone turnpike. It once boasted stables for 'six pairs', providing fresh horses for the coaches. Where dogs are used on signs they are usually heraldic devices, but the Dog and Bear is a rare exception, for its name recalls the old sport of bear-baiting. The well-maintained exterior proudly displays a brilliant royal coat of arms over the door, which commemorates the visit of Queen Anne to the hotel in 1704.

The inn has an established reputation locally for good value, home-cooked food. Among the hearty snacks available are a generous ploughman's lunch, imaginatively filled sandwiches – bacon and smoked chicken – and home-made soup. Main menu choices range from omelettes, liver, bacon and onions, lasagne and steak and kidney pie to chicken balti, whole dressed crab and an interesting salad bowl. Restaurant fare includes steaks, mixed grill, trout, haunch of venison and medallions of pork in Madeira sauce. Sunday roasts are a popular feature. Traditional nursery puddings – spotted dick, for example – and crème brûlée are also on offer. To accompany your meal there are excellent local ales – Master Brew and Spitfire – and a short, varied list of wines. Food is served daily from 12 noon to 2.30 pm and 7 pm to 9.30 pm.

To the rear of the inn is an enclosed sun-trap patio with picnic benches, tubs of plants and colourful hanging baskets in season. Children and dogs are welcome inside and out. The bars are open all day on Monday to Saturday from 11 am to 11 pm and on Sunday from 12 noon to 10.30 pm.

Telephone: 01622 858219.

How to get there: Lenham is located just off the A20, midway between Maidstone and Ashford and 4½ miles from junction 8 of the M20.

Parking: The hotel has a spacious rear car park and the free village car park is adjacent. Village square parking is short stay only.

Length of the walk: 2¼ miles. Map: OS Landranger 189 Ashford and Romney Marsh (inn GR 899522).

This short and easy country stroll follows level farmland and field paths close to the sources of the river Stour, before crossing the busy A20 and ascending the lower slopes of the North Downs to join an open and scenic section of the Pilgrims' Way, affording good views over the village and surrounding rolling countryside. Make sure you allow plenty of time to explore historic Lenham, especially the pretty square and fascinating church.

The Walk

1 From the front entrance of the Dog and Bear head to the right across the village square, passing the bakery and following the Stour

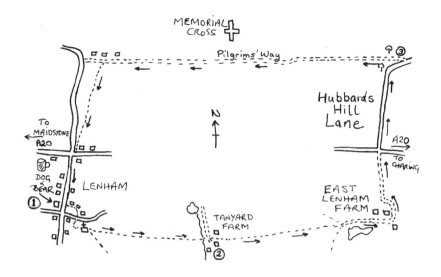

Valley Walk waymarker. The café and garage to your left in the square were once a court room in medieval times and, more recently, a pub called the Chequers. In a few yards enter Church Square, pass through the lychgate into St Mary's churchyard and step inside the splendid 14th-century church. Built of Kentish ragstone and flint, it has Saxon and Norman origins, the former church being burnt down in 1297. It houses some interesting treasures, namely 14th-century wall paintings, an ornately carved Elizabethan pulpit, an unusual priest's chair and a tombstone to Mary Honywood, who died in 1620 aged 92, leaving, unbelievably, 367 descendants from 16 children and 114 grandchildren! Nearby is a magnificent timbered tithe barn, an old mounting block and a 15th-century Wealden hall house that once housed the village forge.

Follow the tarmac path through the churchyard to a wooden kissing-gate, then keep left along a field edge behind houses, disregarding the worn diagonal path (Stour Valley Walk). Pass a yellow marker post and shortly cross a small footbridge in the field corner into the farmyard of Tanyard Farm, noting the old waterpump on a tree. You have just crossed one of the tiny streams that go on to form the river Stour.

2 Walk ahead between the farmhouse and barns, go through a metal gate, then bear slightly left across pastureland to a swing gate and continue half-left to a visible stile on the field edge. Cross a footbridge and proceed straight on through sheep-grazed pasture, soon to pick up a defined track in the field corner leading towards East Lenham Farm. Go through a gate near ponds – one of three sources of the river Stour – and enter the farmyard. Turn left beyond the small old oast house to join the farm drive and follow this attractive tree-lined way out to the busy A20.

Taking great care, cross straight over into Hubbards Hill Lane, signposted 'Warren Street'. Gently ascend on this relatively traffic-free narrow lane for ¼ mile, then as it curves steeply to the right, turn left at the end of metal railings onto a waymarked byway (Pilgrims' Way/ North Downs Way).

3 Follow this established ancient routeway, initially through trees to a gate, then between open fields at the base of the scarp slope of the North Downs. Make use of the welcome bench located in a small fenced area below the large cross etched in the chalk hillside. Measuring 188 ft high and 65 ft wide, it was created in 1922 as a memorial to the 42 local casualties of the First World War. During World War Two it was covered up so as not to be an obvious landmark to enemy aircraft, but was later uncovered, by which time an extra 14 names had to be added to the large granite stones that once stood by the cross. These were removed in 1960 and placed in Lenham churchyard. It is a good place to take in the lovely views over the village.

Continue to a gate, then walk along a metalled access drive, soon to bear off left to a small gate, opposite the drive to Northdown. Bear right along a worn path around the field edge and gradually descend to the A20. Again, carefully cross this fast road and walk down Faversham Road back to the square in Lenham. Just before reaching the square, look out for the old lock-up with its ashlar front and rusticated arch on your right. Originally built in 1723 as a mortuary for the adjoining workhouse (now cottages), it was later used as the village gaol in the late 19th century.

Places of interest nearby

Leeds Castle (3 miles west) is a beautiful, fairy-tale castle built on the site of a manor of a Saxon royal family in the 9th century. Described as 'the loveliest castle in the world', it occupies two small islands in a lake within 500 acres of landscaped parkland. Tel: 01622 765400.

Newnham
The George Inn ✓

Newnham is an unspoilt small village that occupies a single street in an attractive valley on the back slope of the North Downs. Contrary to the meaning of its name – new settlement – the community is very old, possessing the remains of a Norman motte-and-bailey castle and a few fine buildings, notably Calico House, a splendid half-timbered Tudor residence with a pargeted front decorated with flowing leaves painted in terracotta. In the heart of the village street is the church of St Peter and St Paul, opposite which stands the 16th-century George Inn. Built in 1540 as a farm dwelling, it was for a long time part of the church's property, acting as the village brewhouse. Ale was brewed and stored here for the refreshment of the parishioners at church and at parish meetings, and sold at village fairs and celebrations. It became an inn in 1718 and was acquired by the local Shepherd Neame brewery as long ago as 1841.

The mellow brick and tile-hung façade hides a lovingly maintained interior. A series of atmospheric, interconnected rooms are served by a long, wood-panelled bar and feature exposed beams, warming open fires in winter, a rug strewn, polished wooden floor and a delightful mixture of tasteful furnishings, including upholstered mahogany settles, oak refectory tables and comfortable farmhouse chairs. The civilised ambience is enhanced by quality prints and paintings, interesting collections of butterflies, clay pipes and stuffed birds, with added touches like beautiful fresh and dried flower arrangements and candlelit tables.

The George has an enviable reputation for imaginative and varied home-cooked food, attracting a discerning clientele from far and wide – so if you intend dining in the evening you had better book a table. Regular menu items to choose from include favourite snacks like ploughman's lunches, freshly-cut sandwiches and home-made soup, with main dishes such as steak and kidney pie, game pie and rack of lamb with rosemary. The handwritten list of more elaborate daily specials using fresh local produce may include lemon and ginger poussin on a bed of caramelised onions, pot roast pheasant with wine and chestnuts, or fish brochette with piquant sauce. Vegetarians will be delighted with unusual dishes like aduki bean and chestnut loaf. Finish off with rhubarb crumble, chocolate sponge pudding or pineapple cheesecake. Food is served from 12 noon to 2 pm (1.30 pm on Sunday) and 7.30 pm to 10 pm, except on Sunday evening or all day Monday. Excellent Shepherd Neame ales – Master Brew, Spitfire, Bishops Finger, Original Porter (winter) – are available on handpump, alongside a good selection of wines, including four served by the glass.

There is a spacious and peaceful rear garden with picnic benches overlooking sloping, sheep-grazed pastures. Well-behaved children and dogs are welcome inside, and the latter are provided with a drinking bowl in the lobby. The George is open from 10.30 am to 3 pm and 6 pm to 11 pm (Sunday 12 noon to 2 pm and 7 pm to 10.30 pm).

Telephone: 01795 890237.

How to get there: Newnham lies on a rural lane 5 miles south-west of Faversham and is signposted south off the A2, just west of Ospringe outside Faversham. The pub is located opposite the church in the village centre.

Parking: The inn has a small car park.

Length of the walk: 2½ miles. Map: OS Landranger 178 Thames Estuary (inn GR 955576).

This gently undulating and varied walk explores well-waymarked woodland and field paths and the interesting village of Eastling, with its magnificent timbered manor house and 13th-century church. Generally easy going, but be prepared for some mud after rain.

The Walk

1 From the pub turn left along the village street and take the waymarked footpath on your right, opposite Cairn House and close to the village edge and playing field. Shortly, keep left along a worn path, heading uphill through Homefield Wood to reach a clearing. Proceed ahead and keep to the right-hand edge of the clearing to join a good path back into woodland. Disregard the arrowed stile on your right and continue straight on (yellow arrow on tree) through the woodland fringe to a stile. Turn right downhill alongside a fence, ignoring the stile on your right, and remain on this defined, meandering path as it ascends through a narrow stretch of woodland. On reaching an unsigned fork of paths bear right, soon to join an enclosed path between ugly metal fencing – a galvanised alley – leading to a small housing estate. Follow the tarmac path to the lane and turn right into Eastling village.

2 Just beyond Newnham Lane, follow the tarmac path on your left to St Mary's church. Eastling is situated on an ancient way across the North Downs and it is known that the Eslinges, a Jutish tribe, first built a settlement here in the 5th century. It later became an important village, as the Domesday Book records two churches in the parish and no less than four manors. The present church, although significantly restored externally in 1856, dates from the 11th century and features a Norman doorway, some fine box pews and a stone-flagged floor. The magnificent yew tree in the churchyard is 2,000 years old and still full of vigour.

Walk through the church car park and turn right along the lane, soon taking the waymarked path (arrow on telegraph pole) left beyond a pink-washed cottage. If you continue to the junction opposite the Carpenters Arms, take a look at the splendid timbered manor house on your left. It is said to be the second oldest complete building in Kent (dating from 1280) and was the birthplace of Edward Hasted, the eminent 18th-century Kentish historian. Back on

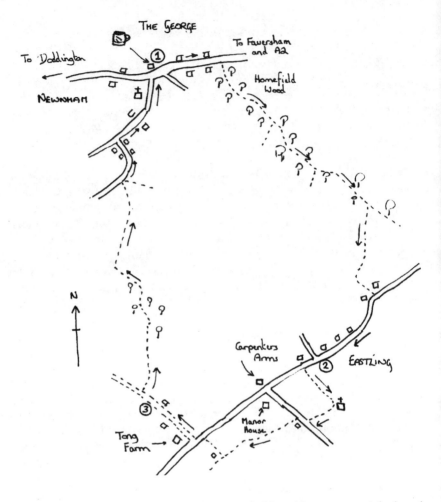

the circuit, follow a short drive, enter a field and keep to its right-hand edge, then head across the field to a stile (there is a white house to the right). Cross a couple of paddocks via stiles, then walk ahead across a broad field towards an old, partly hidden Nissen hut and waymarker post. Turn right to reach a lane, then turn left and almost immediately right along a farm drive, passing the beautifully timbered Tong Farm.

3 Proceed through the farm on a good track, pass some farm cottages, then towards the end of the field on your right, opposite a track on the left, follow a clear path (not waymarked) across the field to enter woodland, just up from the field corner. Your path curves left, becoming more defined as it descends through a tunnel of coppiced trees, shortly reaching a stile and a large field. Turn left uphill along the field edge, soon to bear diagonally right along the line of telegraph poles to the field corner and a lane. Turn right and follow the narrow lane back into Newnham, going through a small estate to a T-junction. Turn right again and soon pass the entrance to a vineyard (where there is a nature trail) and the church to the main village street and the George Inn opposite.

Places of interest nearby

Doddington Place Gardens (1 mile west) are lovely landscaped gardens set in the grounds of an imposing Victorian mansion and cover 10 acres. Of interest are an Edwardian garden, different sorts of rhododendrons and azaleas and a woodland area. Refreshments are available. Open on Wednesdays and during bank holidays from Easter to September. Telephone: 01795 886385. Historic Faversham (5 miles north-east) has the fascinating *Fleur de Lys Heritage Centre,* where a thousand years of the town's history and architecture are shown in award-winning displays and an audio-visual programme. Telephone: 01795 534542. Rare and traditional breeds of farm animals and birds, an adventure playground, museum and farm trail can be found at *Farming World,* set within the magnificent grounds of Nash Court at Boughton (2 miles east of Faversham). Telephone: 01227 751224. At Ospringe on the A2 near Faversham is the famous *Maison Dieu,* a timber-framed hall that stands on the site of a monastic hospital founded by Henry VIII. It now houses a fascinating Heritage Museum and is open on weekend afternoons. Telephone: 01795 534542.

9 Stalisfield Green
The Plough ✓

Nestling beside the green in this unspoilt farming community on the crest of the North Downs is the Plough, a magnificent 15th-century building that enjoys lovely views across the Swale to the Isle of Sheppey. This splendid Kentish hall house was originally a farmhouse before becoming an alehouse in 1745. Today, it is a civilised country pub, attracting a loyal clientele from far and wide for the above average pub food on offer. Inside are two immaculately maintained and welcoming beamed bars, furnished with a comfortable mix of old and new pine, including high-backed settles, pews and farmhouse chairs, and warmed in winter by two open log fires. There is an attractive, light and airy garden room with access to a sheltered patio and peaceful side garden with rustic tables and benches. Various watercolours, prints and old photographs adorn the walls and candles on the tables enhance the relaxing dining ambience.

The Plough is a popular freehouse dispensing a good range of real ales on handpump – Harveys Sussex Bitter, Shepherd Neame Master Brew and Adnams Extra – and offering an interesting choice of wines, including a short, value-for-money list of bin ends, to complement the excellent food. As the pub has a French proprietor/chef, it follows that the food has a distinct Gallic flavour, and even the weekly-changing blackboard menu is written in French. All dishes are freshly-cooked to order and may include starters/snacks like soupe l'oignon, crème de legumes, terrine maison, moules farcie, crevettes sauté à l'ail, crêpe aux fruits de mers or huitres, followed by fillet de boeuf grille, magret de canard, pigeon au sauternes et raisin, confit de canard, carré d'agneau au Romarin and fillet de haddock sauce Mornay. Tarte chocolat and crêpes aux pommes avec sorbet de cassis may appear on the pudding list. Vegetarians can be catered for. Walkers desiring just a light lunchtime snack will not be disappointed and will find home-made soup, ploughman's lunches and a range of sandwiches.

Children are not allowed in the bars and dogs may go inside only if they are on a lead. The adjacent field is set aside for touring caravans. The pub is open from 12 noon to 3 pm every day and from 7 pm to 11 pm on Monday to Saturday evenings. It is closed on Mondays, except for bank holidays, when it closes the Tuesday following. Food is available from 12 noon to 1.45 pm and 7 pm to 9.15 pm.

Telephone: 01795 890256.

How to get there: Stalisfield Green is situated on a country lane 2½ miles north of the A20 Ashford to Maidstone road and is signposted 1 mile north-west of Charing. The Plough is easily located, as it is set back from the green in the centre of this scattered village.

Parking: The pub has its own large car park.

Length of the walk: 4 miles. Map: OS Landranger 189 Ashford and Romney Marsh (inn GR 954530).

This delightful rural circuit explores peaceful, undulating farm-land and woodland paths across the scenic backslope of the North Downs. Very much a get-away-from-it-all ramble to enjoy the open countryside and the varied wildlife that exists on the Downs, as this walk does not take in any cultural diversions like villages and their churches. Generally easy going underfoot.

The Walk

1 On leaving the pub cross the green – which was used for a fairground scene in an episode of the *The Darling Buds of May* – and the village lane, passing the village hall to follow School Lane to a T-junction. Disregard the stile opposite and turn right to climb the waymarked stile on your left. Keep to the left-hand edge of the field, soon to cross a stile in the field corner and descend through Spuckles Wood to a crossing of paths in the base of the valley. At the turn of the century until the 1920s the area was known for charcoal pro-duction, much of the wood originating from coppiced woodland like Spuckles Wood. The charcoal was mainly used to fire hop driers in oasthouses. However, some went to the gunpowder works in Faversham and during the First World War it was sent to France for use as a fuel in the battle areas. Not only did it keep the soldiers warm but, being smokeless, it was not detectable by enemy soldiers.

Turn left in the wooded valley, keeping left as the path forks, and gently climb through the trees to reach a gate on the woodland fringe. Proceed straight ahead along a defined terrace in the pasture, with pretty views down to a fine black-and-white timbered building in the valley bottom, to reach a gate and lane.

2 Cross over and walk along the driveway to Woodsell. Pass in front of the farmhouse, then bear off right on to a stony track which skirts the edge of a field, before curving right through Great Spelty Wood. Keep to the track, gradually descending to à narrow lane in the valley. Turn left, then shortly climb the arrowed stile on your right and bear half-left across the field to a stile. Maintain course uphill to a further stile on the edge of Hazel Wood. Follow the clear path left and soon curve right uphill through scrub and mixed trees to a stile and an open field. Bear diagonally left across the field, soon to locate a waymarked stile in a fence, then maintain direction through a broad field towards two long sheds near a farmhouse, eventually reaching a lane.

3 Turn left along the lane, then head steeply downhill to a cross-roads in the valley and go straight across, up a sharp wooded hill, signposted 'Stalisfield Green'. At the top of the hill, turn left with a fingerpost through double gates into the driveway to Holbeam House. Where the drive bears right beyond garages, keep ahead to an arrowed gate. Proceed half-right across pasture to a stile – with open views over rolling downland – then turn right along a grassy path, which soon curves sharp left between large, open arable fields, heading towards woodland.

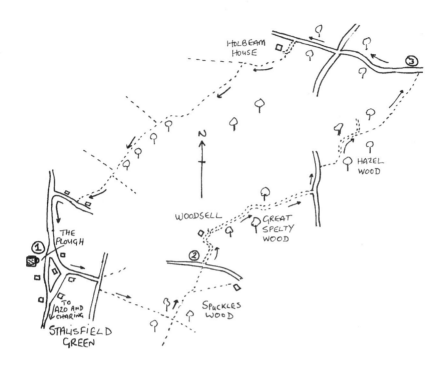

Cross a stile on the edge of trees at the field edge, and proceed straight ahead on the clear path to a further stile. Your route maintains the same direction along the left-hand edge of two more fields beside woodland to a stile, then bears diagonally half-right through pasture to a stile located midway between two dwellings. Turn right onto a lane, then in 150 yards, at a T-junction, turn left for the short stroll back to the Plough.

Places of interest nearby

Doddington Place Gardens (4½ miles north) are extensive landscaped gardens with spectacular woodland, formal terraces, an Edwardian rock garden, late summer borders and delightful views. Refreshments are available. Open Wednesdays and bank holidays from Easter to September. Telephone: 01795 886101.

10 Westwell
The Wheel Inn

The pretty little village of Westwell nestles beneath the North Downs amid some of the most peaceful and beautiful pastoral landscape in the county. Set well off the beaten track, it comprises a delightful collection of buildings, including attractive cottages, an old mill, a modern rectory and an interesting church, set around two small greens, one with a fine group of large chestnut trees. Standing opposite is the brick-built, virginia creeper-clad Wheel Inn which dates back some 250 years, although an alehouse is believed to have existed here as long as the church. The unusual name is derived from the Catherine Wheel, an ancient inn name which commemorates the martyrdom of St Catherine, bound to a wheel. If you look carefully at the wheel on the signboard you will notice that not all the spokes are of the same colour. During the last war, New Zealanders, who were stationed in nearby Eastwell Park, were frequent visitors to the inn, and it is said that they had spent enough money in the pub to have bought at least two of the spokes, so a couple were painted in the New Zealand colours.

46

The Wheel Inn is an unpretentious village local with three homely interconnecting rooms, featuring old tiled floors, warming open fires in the colder months, an interesting mix of old-fashioned furniture and small collections of teapots and time-worn black and white photographs. Part of the bar is given over to a pool table and there is also a small cosy dining room.

Owned by the Shepherd Neame brewery, the inn offers well-kept Master Brew, Spitfire, Bishops Finger and, in winter, Porter ales on handpump, plus a selection of draught lagers and bottled beers. The straightforward bar food is home-cooked and good value, with lunchtime fare like ploughman's lunches, freshly-cut sandwiches, farmhouse pie, gammon steak and breaded plaice or cod. Regular evening extras include steaks, salads, chicken Kiev and marinated chicken breast in lemon and black pepper, whereas the daily specials board may list steak and kidney pie, tuna, prawn and pasta bake and chilli con carne. Vegetarians can choose from vegetable chilli and spinach and mushroom lasagne. Those with hearty walking appetites can indulge in a pudding, such as Bakewell tart, apple pie, treacle pudding or hot chocolate fudge cake. There are popular roast lunches on a Sunday and occasional Malaysian gourmet evenings. Food is available from 12 noon to 2 pm and 7 pm to 9 pm, except Wednesday evenings.

To the side of the pub there is a huge sheltered garden with shrub and flower borders, mature trees, a bat and trap pitch and picnic benches – ideal for summer sipping. Both children and dogs are welcome indoors, if permission is asked first. If you wish to linger in the area longer, the pub offers accommodation in three letting bedrooms.

Telephone: 01223 712430.

How to get there: Westwell is 4 miles from Ashford. It is located 1½ miles north-west of the A20 between Ashford and Charing and 1½ miles south of the A252 Charing to Canterbury road, the turning being 1 mile west of Challock. The Wheel Inn will be found by the green in the centre of the village.

Parking: The inn has its own car park.

Length of the walk: 4½ miles. Map: OS Landranger 189 Ashford and Romney Marsh (inn GR 989475).

Beginning from a 1,000 year old village, this picturesque circuit follows the even more ancient Pilgrims' Way through mature broadleaf woodland, before ascending to the top of the North Downs. The return route traverses open, sheep-grazed pastures affording panoramic views across farms and villages to the market town of Ashford. The walk is particularly attractive in spring when the woodland edges are full of wild flowers and the trees alive with birds.

The Walk

1 From the pub car park go across the crossroads and follow the lane beside the Old School House, signposted 'Challock Lees' and 'Faversham'. However, if you are interested in churches, why not first turn right to visit the church of St Mary, which, although rather drab from the outside, possesses a splendid Early English interior, notably some fine stone columns and a remarkable stone-vaulted chancel. Back on the route and just past the last house on your left, look out for a hidden concrete footpath sign in the hedge by a telegraph pole and enter a large open field. Keep left along the hedge for a few yards, then strike out diagonally right on a clear path through the arable field, gently ascending to reach a stile and a lane.

Turn right, then shortly bear left at a byway fingerpost to join the North Downs Way (Pilgrims' Way), a metalled track that soon passes Pilgrims Cottage. Your route becomes a delightful wide path along the base of Westwell Downs, passing through the edge of Charing Beech Hangers – a mature ash, oak and beech woodland that is a Site of Special Scientific Interest and haven to a wealth of fauna and flora. This sheltered section of the North Downs Way also affords cameo views across the Weald and the welcoming sight of 'Arthurs Seat', a perfectly positioned bench which allows you to savour the rural scene. Within a mile pass a house called Beechside, keeping ahead with the red North Downs Way marker, and shortly join a concrete access road to Beacon Hill Quarry (entrance to your right).

2 As this road curves left, bear off right with the red arrowed post and begin the steady ascent on an old sunken track up the scarp slope of the North Downs. At the top, pass a board informing you that you are near gliding club property and keep to the fenced path alongside coppiced woodland. In springtime you should see bluebells and wood anemones and later colourful foxgloves beneath the tree canopy. Eventually reach a lane and turn right (yellow arrow), climbing gradually uphill to a waymarked stile on your left.

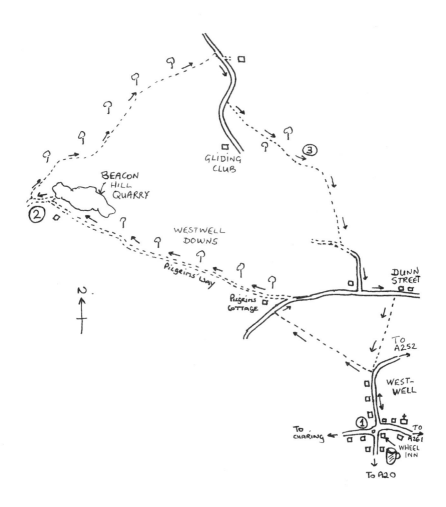

Cross the stile, then bear half-right through pasture towards a telegraph pole and keep to its right, soon to locate a stile visible ahead on the fringe of Wrotham Wood. Proceed through the wood on a worn path to a stile, then continue straight ahead across sheep pasture (arrowed post) to a further stile and pause to enjoy the far-reaching views across Ashford and along the face of the North Downs. In summer skylarks can be seen singing high above the downs and you may spot a kestrel hovering in search of prey.

3 Bear slightly right towards the unfolding vista to reach a further stile, which soon comes into view. Maintain direction downhill across

A typical downland path.

lush pasture, soon to climb a stile flanking a gate and, in a few yards, bear left along a metalled track. At a T-junction with the Pilgrims' Way – an ancient track that has been in continuous use since Neolithic times some 5,000 years ago – turn left and shortly take the way-marked footpath right, opposite Dunn Street Cottage. Keep left-handed along the field edge, then descend on a defined path along a line of telegraph poles towards Westwell and soon pick up your outward route in the field corner to return to the Wheel Inn.

Places of interest nearby

Hothfield Common (2 miles south) is the remains of an ancient, and once much larger, heath and bog complex. Now a nature reserve, it is home to a great number of mosses, orchids, butterflies and dragonflies. There are nature trails and a picnic site. *Godinton House* (1 mile further south) is a fine Jacobean mansion with collections of European porcelain, furniture and portraits, and 18th-century topiary gardens. Open Easter and Sundays from June to September. Telephone: 01233 620773. Near Eastwell Park (1½ miles east) and adjoining Eastwell Lake are the ruins of *St Mary's church*, comprising principally of a Perpendicular tower with angle buttresses.

⑪ Hernhill
The Red Lion

The neat and attractive village of Hernhill nestles among orchards on a hilltop at the furthest extent of the North Downs backslope, looking across the Graveney marshes to the North Kent coast near Whitstable. Framing the delightful, rectangular green in the charming village centre are the fine 15th-century Perpendicular church of St Michael and the adjacent Manor House with its half-timbered north-end wing standing in the churchyard, a picturesque row of 19th-century cottages, some farmyard oasts and the handsome half-timbered Red Lion. Built in the 14th century, this splendid example of a Wealden hall house has two wings projecting in front of the main building and a roof supported by curved brackets.

As one would expect from such a historic building, the interior is full of character, with the heavily beamed and flagstoned narrow bar featuring some exposed brick and some pine tongue and groove walls, winter log fires, plenty of rustic pine tables and chairs and various bygone farming tools and implements adorning the walls and ceilings. There is generally a cosy and bustling atmosphere in both the bar and the beamed upstair restaurant. On fine days the rear garden, complete with pétanque and bat and trap pitches and a children's play area, is a popular place to enjoy a drink, as are the appealing front picnic benches which offer relaxing views across the green to the church.

The Red Lion is a welcoming freehouse dispensing a good range of real ales, such as Shepherd Neame Master Brew, Fuller's London Pride, Boddingtons, Morland Old Speckled Hen and M&B Highgate Dark Ale, as well as Theobalds scrumpy cider, a range of country fruit wines and a short list of wines by the bottle and glass. Generous helpings of home-cooked bar food include all the favourite snacks – ploughman's lunches, sandwiches, steak and kidney pudding, filled jacket potatoes – and changing blackboard specials like lentil soup, stir-fried beef, salad Niçoise, salmon and spring onion fishcakes and pork fillet with apricot sauce. Evening restaurant additions may include seafood carbonara, chicken Red Lion served with cream and peppers, lamb fillet with honey and mint sauce and breast of duck with redcurrant and damson sauce. Vegetarians can choose from spinach bake, hazelnut and vegetable loaf and vegetable lasagne. Food is served from 12 noon to 2.30 pm and 7 pm to 10 pm, except in the restaurant on Sunday evenings.

Children are welcome inside, away from the bar, and dogs are only allowed in if on leads. Overnight accommodation is available. The bar is open from 11 am to 3 pm and 6 pm to 11 pm (Sunday 12 noon to 3 pm and 7 pm to 10.30 pm).

Telephone: 01227 751207.

How to get there: Hernhill lies 2½ miles off the A2 between Canterbury and Faversham, via Dunkirk or Boughton Street (1 mile east of the M2 at junction 7). The village can also be reached from the A299, the M2 (junction 7) to Whitstable road, by turning at the Highstreet roundabout, then continuing via Dargate. It is well sign-posted.

Parking: There is a car park to the rear of the pub.

Length of the walk: 2 miles. Map: OS Landranger 179 Canterbury and East Kent (inn GR 065607).

This gently undulating short stroll explores well-waymarked footpaths that criss-cross the wealth of apple and pear orchards that surround the charming village of Hernhill. The focus of the walk, apart from visiting the splendid parish church, is Mount Ephraim Gardens, a magnificent Edwardian garden with rose terraces, a small lake and a Japanese rock garden, among other delights. Generally easy going underfoot and good views can be enjoyed across the Swale to the Isle of Sheppey.

The Walk

1 From the front entrance to the pub turn left along Crockham Lane, then just beyond the last house on the village fringe, take the waymarked footpath (concrete post) into a field, which may well be under strawberry cultivation. If this is the case, follow the left-hand edge of the field round to a stile bridge over a ditch and enter an orchard. Turn right, then in a few yards at a fork of paths, bear left between lines of pear trees (arrowed) and keep left on reaching the orchard edge, soon to climb a stile in the fence to your right. Turn left along the field edge to a track and follow it right (orchard to left), then at the perimeter of the orchard bear left, shortly to cross a stile.

Bear diagonally left downhill through pasture, with good views towards Mount Ephraim House, to reach a stile beside a green metal gate. Follow the orchard edge, climb an arrowed stile on your right and head straight across pasture, uphill to a stile, and enter another orchard. Turn right with the waymarker arrow and proceed along the orchard edge, then where the perimeter hedge bears right, veer off left along a defined path between trees – a delightful path in springtime with the colour and heady perfume of blossom. Continue into a further orchard, keeping ahead on a grassy path to shortly enter a third orchard, finally reaching a lane via a gap in the hedge by a footpath fingerpost.

2 Cross straight over to follow a high-hedged metalled driveway, soon to pass a converted oast house. Descend and climb on the tarmac route, then just before a ruined brick building, turn right to cross a stile beside a gate. Proceed straight ahead along a grassy path through an orchard, affording far-reaching views across the Swale. Climb a further stile and turn right down a narrow fenced path towards Mount Ephraim House, visible ahead. Shortly, ascend to a lane, bearing left then immediately right into the entrance to Mount Ephraim Gardens.

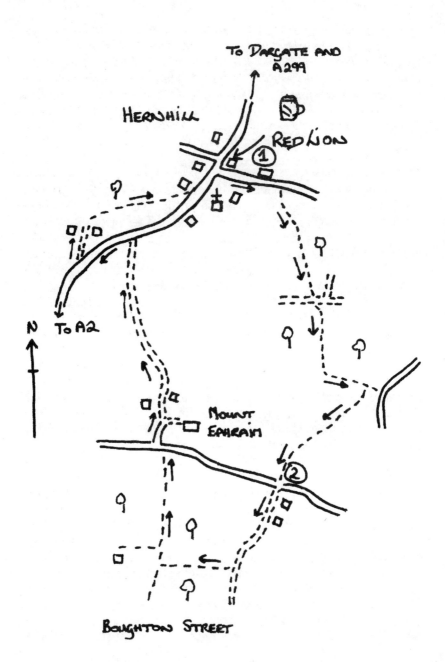

To Dargate and A299

Hernhill

Red Lion

①

To A2

N

Mount Ephraim

②

Boughton Street

If you are walking this way between mid-April and September, why not add some further interest to your expedition by strolling round these beautifully maintained gardens. As well as rose terraces, there are herbaceous borders, intricate topiary work, a woodland area with rhododendrons, an extensive Japanese rock garden and a vineyard.

To continue the walk, keep left at the fork arrowed to the car park, just inside the entrance to the gardens, and remain on this metalled drive to reach a road. Turn left downhill for 100 yards, then opposite a white weatherboarded house, take the waymarked path up the driveway to a house called Claremont and pass through a narrow gate into an orchard. Proceed straight on, uphill towards Hernhill church, to reach a stile and the road through the village. Turn left back to the village green and the Red Lion, but make time to visit the church on the way, as it has on sale an excellent church guide, highlighting the history of both the building and the village.

Places of interest nearby

Mount Ephraim Gardens are open in the afternoons daily between mid-April and September and on Sundays during October for the autumn colours. Teas are available daily and there is a craft centre on Sundays. Telephone: 01227 751496. Just outside Boughton Street (1½ miles south-west) and set within the magnificent grounds of Nash Court is *Farming World* where you can see rare and traditional breeds of farm animals, birds and Shire horses. An excellent family attraction with an adventure playground, farm trails, a museum, a picnic area and refreshments. Open all year. Telephone: 01227 751224. *Church Woods* outside Blean (4½ miles east) is one of the largest single areas of ancient oak woodland in Britain and is a conservation area with a car park and public footpaths. At Honey Hill (½ mile north of Blean) is *Blean Bird Park* housing Britain's largest parrot collection, as well as owls, toucans, a pets corner, play area and refreshments. Open daily from March to November. Telephone: 01227 471666.

Chilham
The Woolpack Inn

Chilham is probably Kent's prettiest village and ranks high among the most romantic and most visited villages in England. At its heart is a striking and picturesque square fringed with charming half-timbered Tudor houses, a fine Jacobean mansion hidden behind an impressive castle gate and the 13th-century flintstone church of St Mary. Beyond this perfect village scene, which positively teems with visitors in the summer months, three attractive cottage-lined streets radiate off the hill into the Stour valley.

At the bottom of the High Street is the pink-washed Woolpack Inn, an ancient hostelry built in 1422 and with tenancy records dating back to 1428. Facing the inn is Hatfield House, a large Tudor building that was once owned by a wealthy wool merchant and is probably the reason why the Woolpack is named as such. Legends abound in the village regarding the inn, notably the story about a tunnel, large enough to take a coach and horses, linking the cellar to Chilham Castle and used to bring ale for banquets to the castle, or to transport prisoners from the castle to the inn, which is thought to have once been a courthouse. More likely, however, is the tale of the friendly resident ghost – a grey lady who appears in the front bedroom, standing by the open fireplace. During the coaching era the inn became a popular staging post. In keeping with its age, the well refurbished oak-beamed bar boasts a huge inglenook fireplace with a welcoming log fire in winter, dark pine tongue and groove walls adorned with sporting scene prints, and a collection of copper jugs hanging from the central beam. There is also a separate, attractive and equally beamed restaurant.

The inn is one of the five Shepherd Neame Invicta Country Inns and dispenses their Master Brew, Best Bitter and Spitfire real ales on handpump. The well-stocked bar also serves a good range of lagers, bottled beers and malt whiskies. Blackboards display the choice of home-cooked dishes that are available at both lunchtime and in the evenings. Options may include smoked trout salad, melon and prawn cocktail and baked avocado and Stilton for starters, followed by Woolpack mixed grill, lamb solfrido, chicken curry, lambs' liver and bacon, steak and mushroom pie and grilled salmon with dill. Lighter bites include ploughman's lunches, sandwiches (not evenings), filled jacket potatoes and ham, egg and chips. If you have room, round off your meal with a home-made dessert, such as charlotte rousse, crème brûlée or bread and butter pudding. Restaurant fare features the likes of Dover sole, marinated lamb cutlets, fruits de mer and a choice of steaks. Food is available daily from 12 noon to 2 pm and 7 pm to 9 pm.

The Woolpack offers overnight accommodation in 13 en suite bedrooms, some of which occupy converted stables and a small building opposite, formerly a garage, but originally a workhouse for the homeless. For al fresco drinking there is an enclosed rear courtyard and paved terrace with picnic benches. Both dogs and children are welcome in the bar, which is open from 11 am to 3 pm and 6 pm to 11 pm (Sunday 12 noon to 3 pm and 7 pm to 10.30 pm). Telephone: 01227 730208 or 730351.

How to get there: Chilham is located close to the junction of the A252 from Charing and the A28 Canterbury to Ashford road, 6½ miles south-west of Canterbury. The Woolpack is situated 100 yards from the village square at the bottom of the High Street.

Parking: The inn has a car park to the rear. Alternatively, park in the square or in the free village car park.

Length of the walk: 3 miles. Map: OS Landranger 179 Canterbury and East Kent or 189 Ashford and Romney Marsh (inn GR 071536).

After a leisurely stroll through this most charming village, where you are bound to linger longer than intended, this easy and well-waymarked circuit follows parts of the North Downs Way and the Stour Valley Walk through the valley of the Great Stour. Plenty of historical interest to explore and some delightful views to admire.

The Walk

1 Leave the inn and turn left up the High Street into the beautiful village square, passing Burgoyne House – originally a farmhouse built in the 1300s – and the Butcher's Shop, now a gift shop and one of the oldest shops in the country, along the way. Further exploration in the square will reveal the parish church with its interesting relics and monuments (there is an excellent village guide for sale), splendid half-timbered Tudor buildings and Chilham Castle, set in 25 acres of gardens with formal terraces and magnificent views. Keep left through the square and walk down School Hill beside the walls to the castle grounds.

At the bottom, keep ahead along Mountain Street (North Downs Way), a metalled lane that skirts the castle grounds, affording cameo views of the fine Jacobean mansion, the remains of the Norman castle and the lake, which has been the site of a heronry for the past 800 years. On reaching the hamlet of Mountain Street, pass Heron Manor – a typical Kentish black and white timbered dwelling built in 1480 – and Monkton Manor, then turn left (hidden footpath sign) onto a narrow path beside April Cottage to enter a field.

2 Bear diagonally right on a defined path to a stile in a hedgerow, then proceed along the right-hand edge of pasture to a further stile. Maintain direction, soon to bear left towards a yellow-topped post in the field and shortly cross a footbridge over the river Great Stour to reach the busy A28. Taking extreme care, cross straight over and turn left along the verge, soon to turn right along the drive to East Stour Farm. Climb a stile beside a gate, pass beneath the railway bridge and, shortly, cross the stile on your left beside a red-painted gate.

Join a splendid path which gently ascends the valley side, affording delightful views across the valley to the hilltop church and castle in Chilham. At a crossing of tracks, continue ahead with the waymarker to join the Stour Valley Walk, a long distance footpath which links

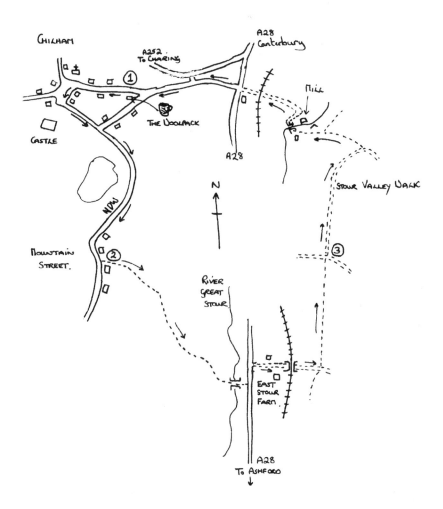

Lenham (near Maidstone) to Pegwell Bay, a distance of some 58 miles.

3 You are now following a wide track – Old Wye Lane – an old route from Wye to Canterbury, which continues to gradually climb to the top of Julliberrie Downs, offering extensive views. Keep to the path as it curves right and begins to descend, then look out for a stile on your left. Beyond the stile, follow the Stour Valley Walk link path along the right-hand edge of a field, descending to a copse and junction of paths. Nearby is a Neolithic long barrow – Julliberrie's Grave – which takes its name from Juilius Laberius, one of Caesar's captains, who died here fighting for Rome in 54 BC.

Disregard the footpath 'FP 16' and proceed downhill through the copse to reach the Great Stour river and Chilham Water Mill. Built in the 19th century and consisting of five floors, this fine white-painted weatherboarded mill was beautifully restored in 1960 by the Mid Kent Water Company who own it and enjoys a picturesque position. Go over the river and follow the metalled access road, soon to cross the railway line at a level crossing and reach the A28 beside a garage. Proceed straight across and follow the lane as it bears left back to the Woolpack Inn and the village.

Places of interest nearby

Chilham Castle Gardens, laid out by 'Capability' Brown, are open daily between Easter and mid-October and flying displays of birds of prey are held most days. Telephone: 01227 730319. The tiny hamlet of *Godmersham* (2½ miles south) has a simple Norman church and Godmersham House (not open) was where Jane Austen wrote *Pride and Prejudice.* Historic *Chartham* (2½ miles north-east) has a typical village green surrounded by attractive houses and a 13th-century church which is famed for its magnificent oak roof and splendid brasses of medieval rectors, also one of a crusader dated 1306.

13 Wye ✓
The New Flying Horse

Nestling at the foot of the North Downs, Wye is an attractive and bustling village that is famed for its college, which was founded in 1428 by Archbishop Kempe as a seminary college for priests, before becoming a grammar school and finally an agricultural college for the University of London in 1900. Origins of the village date from pre-Roman times and it was once a Royal Manor and a market town. Some well preserved 16th-century timber-framed houses line the pretty streets that radiate out from the 13th-century parish church and Church Street has a distinct Georgian atmosphere.

One of the oldest buildings in the village is the former Flying Horse Inn, located opposite the college entrance. It was an inn from 1450 to 1956 before becoming a hostel for college students, but its name lives on at the New Flying Horse, a long, white-painted and partly tile-hung building, situated around the corner in Upper Bridge Street. This was originally a row of six cottages, the oldest pre-dating 1700, that were gradually integrated over the years to become a coaching inn around 1750. The spick and span bars are popular with students, locals and visitors alike, the long and cosy main bar and adjacent dining area featuring a large open fireplace, dark beams, copper-topped tables, darkwood furniture and attractive watercolours of local scenes and buildings. The separate, neat lounge bar boasts a few comfortable armchairs and French doors leading out to the splendid sun-trap patio with tasteful wrought-iron furniture and to the extensive lawned garden – the perfect spot for summer al fresco drinking and barbecues.

The inn is one of Shepherd Neame's Invicta Country Inns, offering their Master Brew, Spitfire and Bishops Finger real ales on draught, alongside Scrumpy Jack cider, a good choice of lagers and a short, interesting list of wines, including a value-for-money wine of the month promotion. Home-cooked bar food draws a loyal clientele, the regularly changing blackboard menu listing dishes like watercress soup, grilled goats' cheese and avocado and smoked chicken for starters, followed by vegetable stir-fry, steak and kidney pie, pork and pepper casserole and spicy roast poussin. A separate pudding board may highlight apple crumble, double chocolate mousse and pear and almond flan. Imaginative evening restaurant fare could include seafood pasta, warm salad of scallops and bacon, rack of lamb with grain mustard sauce, or pork fillet with prunes, cider and cream. Sandwiches, soup and ploughman's lunches are available at lunchtime for those requiring a light snack. Food is served daily from 12 noon to 2 pm and 6.30 pm (7 pm on Sunday) to 9.15 pm.

The inn offers accommodation in six smartly refurbished mainbuilding bedrooms and four in a converted stable block, all with en suite facilities. Both dogs and children are allowed in the bars and overnight. The bar is open from 11 am to 3 pm and 6 pm to 11 pm (Sunday 12 noon to 3 pm and 7 pm to 10.30 pm).

Telephone: 01233 812297.

How to get there: Wye is signposted 1 mile off the A28 Ashford to Canterbury road, 3 miles north-east of Ashford. The inn is situated at the eastern end of the village, beyond Church Street and the library at the end of Bridge Street.

Parking: The inn has a good sized rear car park. Alternatively, park in the free village car park near the church.

Length of the walk: 4½ miles. Map: OS Landranger 179 Canterbury and East Kent or 189 Ashford and Romney Marsh (inn GR 055466).

Having explored a few of the attractive village streets, this undulating ramble follows the well-waymarked North Downs Way and the Stour Valley Walk to the top of the Downs. Delightful rural tracks and bridleways dip and gently climb to the top of the Wye Downs for magnificent long distance views towards the Romney Marsh and the sea. One steep climb and descent.

The Walk

1 On leaving the inn turn left along Upper Bridge Street and take the first turning right into Church Street, a picturesque street that beautifully frames the 12th-century parish church. Enter the church-yard and follow the diagonal path right towards Wye College build-ings, waymarked 'North Downs Way'. Pass beside allotments, then between college buildings to cross Olantigh Road into Occupation Road, which gently ascends between laboratories and nurseries towards the Downs.

Tarmac gives way to a stony track – Wibberley Way – beyond a gate. At a waymarker post, bear off left with the Stour Valley Walk logo to cross an open field on a worn path to a stile and pass through a copse to a lane. Cross the lane and the stile beyond and steadily climb, bearing off left before a brick building and communications mast to a stile into woodland. Shortly, cross a further lane, then at the woodland fringe turn right along the edge of a large field, soon to follow the defined path as it veers diagonally left across the field, climbing uphill to a stile – a good place to pause to savour the view across the Stour valley. Steeply ascend through a copse to a stile at the top of the Downs and proceed straight ahead across pasture to another stile. Maintain direction, passing several horse jumps to reach a stile flanking a gate.

2 Join a grass track and soon merge with a stony track, then keep right at a junction of five routes to follow a hedged trackway. In 100 yards, pass Marriage Farm – meaning farm on a boundary ridge – and descend to a gate. Remain on the track downhill into a combe, with the beautiful, rolling Crundale Downs and the isolated Crundale church a peaceful sight away to your left. On reaching a junction of paths, keep ahead (blue arrow), uphill through a copse, on a good track that soon curves right to a fork of ways. Follow the right-hand arrowed bridleway which gently climbs through splendid mixed woodland, eventually leaving trees to reach a gate. Continue to a junction of paths at two gates and bear left through the smaller gate,

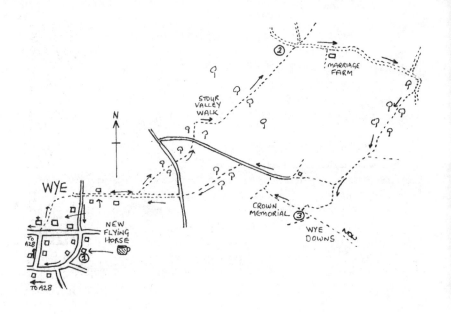

keeping to the field edge to a further arrowed gate. Proceed round the field edge, pass through two further gates, then keep right-handed with breathtaking views beginning to unfold ahead of you.

3 Now on the crest of the North Downs, go through a gate and turn right across a stile to join the North Downs Way, then walk across pitted grassland to an information board positioned above the Wye Crown, a hill carving etched into the chalk downland. This is the symbol of the ancient Royal Manor of Wye and was carved in June 1902 by Wye College students to commemorate the coronation of King Edward VII. A welcome bench encourages you to linger to absorb the fine view across the Vale of the Great Stour and the Kent and Sussex Wealds. The chalk grassland is rich in fauna and flora, notably many rare orchids, wild flowers, herbs and butterflies.

Suitably refreshed, continue along the crest of the Downs, climb a stile beside a gate (North Downs Way), then negotiate two more stiles to reach a lane. Turn left downhill, shortly to take the arrowed path left and descend steeply through woodland off the scarp slope to a gate. Continue ahead, cross a lane and soon rejoin the outward route, back through the Wye College complex to Olantigh Road. Turn left into the village, then at a crossroads (telephone box), go straight over into Upper Bridge Street, back to the inn.

Wye church.

Places of interest nearby

At Brook (2 miles south) is the *Wye College Agricultural Museum* which houses a comprehensive collection of farm implements and tools in a preserved late 14th-century barn and an early 19th-century oast house. Telephone: 01233 812401. *St Mary's church* in Brook boasts a remarkable set of 13th-century wall paintings depicting scenes from the Nativity and the life of Christ. Beautifully located *Crundale church* dates from the 12th century and contains a fine carved slab in memory of a 15th-century rector. *Willesborough Windmill* at Willesborough near Ashford (4 miles south) is a smock mill that has recently been restored to its former glory as a working museum. Open on weekend afternoons from April to October. Telephone: 01233 629165.

14 Bodsham Green
The Timber Batts Inn

The tiny and remote hamlet of Bodsham Green lies in outstanding North Downs countryside amid undulating ridges and dry valleys that are a delight to explore, especially on foot. The ideal starting point for a peaceful ramble in this unspoilt area is the Timber Batts Inn, a 15th-century building which dominates this isolated place. A farming settlement has existed here since before 1086, but the inn was built in 1485 for the bailiff of the Honywood Estate to reside in. Between 1600 and 1780 the building was occupied by tenant farmers who grew hops, some of which were used by the manor of Elmsted and Bodsham to brew beer. This was administered to the poor of the parish, which by 1700 numbered 30, and by 1780 the manor granted the farmer an ale and cider licence to serve those people living within the parish. With such poor roads and so few travellers, there was no need to sell outside the boundary, and it was not until 1833 that, with improved communications, the pub began to serve the general public. The inn was given the name the Prince of Wales and continued to farm the surrounding land until 1859. It remained part of the estate until 1960 and was uniquely named in 1963 after a nearby timber yard producing timber batts.

Despite being altered and refurbished over the years, the large open-plan bar retains a rustic character with a wealth of exposed beams, a large brick fireplace, a mix of furniture – pine pews and farmhouse chairs – various copper and brass artefacts and rural bygones. A separate area houses the pool table. Although it is hard to find, the pub can become busy with those who do track it down, especially the splendid sunny, south-facing terrace which enjoys lovely rural views.

The Timber Batts is a freehouse serving regular real ales – Shepherd Neame Master Brew and Wadworth 6X – and a guest brew like King and Barnes Sussex Bitter. Straightforward home-cooked bar food listed on a large blackboard menu ranges from hearty snacks like sandwiches and ploughman's lunches to liver and bacon, steak and kidney pie, sweet and sour chicken, ham, egg and chips and fish cooked in beer batter. Weekend and evening extras may include half-shoulder of lamb, steaks and local game in season. The vegetarian menu may offer macaroni cheese and vegetable curry. The pudding menu often features treacle sponge, spotted dick and apple pie. Food is available from 12 noon to 2 pm and 7 pm to 10 pm.

Well-behaved dogs and children are welcome inside, the latter having their own menu to choose from. The pub is open from 12 noon to 2.30 pm and 7 pm to 11 pm and is closed on Mondays, except bank holidays.

Telephone: 01233 750237.

How to get there: Bodsham Green lies amid narrow country lanes, 4 miles east of Wye, via Hastingleigh, and 2½ miles from the B2068 (Stone Street) between Canterbury and junction 11 of the M20 near Hythe.

Parking: The inn has a large rear car park and a few spaces to the front.

Length of the walk: 3¼ miles. Map: OS Landranger 179 Canterbury and East Kent or 189 Ashford and Romney Marsh (inn GR 111457).

Those in search of peace and quiet will find this delightful rural ramble most enjoyable. Scenic pasture, farmland and woodland paths meander across unspoilt, rolling downland, affording good country views. There are few taxing hills and the ground is generally firm underfoot but some field and woodland paths may be muddy after wet weather.

The Walk

1 On leaving the front door of the pub turn right alongside the building to follow the arrowed footpath along a metalled farm drive-way to Great Holt Farm. In a short distance cross a waymarked stile beside a gate on your left and keep to a defined path across broad fields, passing between telegraph poles, with splendid valley views. Climb a stile close to a metal gate (arrowed), then bear diagonally right across pasture to a stile at the top of the field – a peaceful spot that enjoys a rural outlook towards Elmstead church, visible above the trees. Go over the stile on your right by a gate and proceed along the left-hand edge of a field to a stile and narrow lane.

2 Cross straight over into the driveway to Podlinge Farm, pass an old pond, then bear left with the drive to go through a gate, located between stables and a garage/outbuilding. Walk across the edge of the garden to a stile flanking a gate near a caravan, then follow a narrow overgrown path between trees – you may have to enter the adjoining field and walk along its edge before rejoining the path, via the fence, at a more convenient spot. Eventually, go through a gate at the end of the trees (not waymarked) and continue straight ahead, downhill across a field to pass through a wide break in a line of beech trees on your left into the next field. Walk along the right-hand edge of the field, with Waltham church visible on the hill in front of you, ῳ reach a fence stile.

Bear diagonally left downhill across grassland to locate a worn path through scrub, leading to a wire fence in a field corner. Step over the fence and proceed half-right towards the tunnel greenhouses on the hill. Pass through a gap between fields and maintain direction to reach an arrowed bridleway post on the field edge. Turn left along the clear path around the field edge, eventually reaching a small wooden gate.

3 Continue ahead on a worn path through a delightful grassy valley between woodlands and soon keep left along the edge of the trees to a gate on the fringe of Bavinge Wood. Nestling among the undulating and picturesque folds of the North Downs, this isolated spot is truly miles from any significant village or town and it is worth lingering

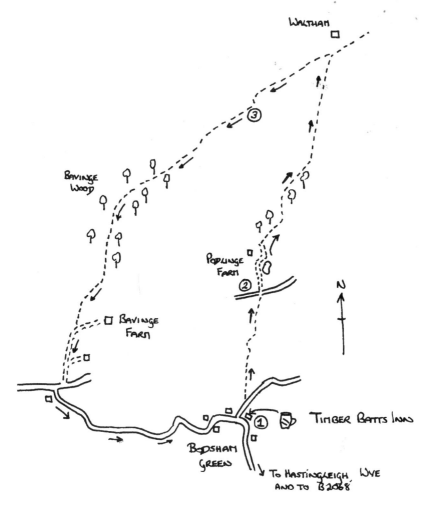

awhile – under the lone tree to your right is a good spot – to savour the peace and quiet, with the exception of the birdsong and the rustling of the trees. Ascend steadily through the wood and emerge out onto an open field. Cross the centre of the field (blue arrow) towards a barn and silos, visible ahead. Shortly, join a metalled farm drive and follow it to a narrow lane. Turn right, then immediately left at a junction and remain on this relatively traffic-free rural lane, as it winds its way for ¾ mile back to the hamlet of Bodsham Green and the Timber Batts Inn.

15 Brabourne
The Five Bells ✓

Tucked beneath the Pilgrims' Way among orchards and a tangle of narrow lanes at the base of the North Downs, the tiny hamlet of Brabourne consists of an attractive single street with an unexpectedly awe-inspiring church at one end and a country inn – the Five Bells – at the other. This welcoming pub is a popular destination both with walkers diverting off the North Downs Way in search of refreshment and with car-bound travellers exploring this delightfully rural and unspoilt area of Kent. The oldest part of this neat, white-painted building dates from 1530 and was thought to have been a workhouse before becoming a pub in the 1700s.

The well-maintained interior has been modernised and refurbished over the years, a large central bar, constructed of brick and black-painted barrels, serving a pleasant open-plan layout of interconnecting rooms. Among the interesting features are some original oak beams, a large inglenook fireplace with heavy overmantel beam and warming winter log fire, a comfortable collection of darkwood furniture and cushioned wall bench seating, and numerous prints and brassware.

The Five Bells is a freehouse serving four real ales – Courage Best and Directors, Shepherd Neame Master Brew and Ruddles County – plus a good range of draught lagers, stouts, bottled beers and a short list of wines. The printed bar menu highlights a comprehensive range of pub meals, such as smoked trout, potted shrimps and garlic mushrooms to start, followed by various steaks or grills and home-made main dishes, like veal masala, chicken bonne femme, steak and kidney pie, breast of duck and fisherman's pie. The vegetarian section offers a choice of omelettes, provençale nut Wellington and mush-room and nut fettuccini. Walkers happy to sample just a snack will find a selection of sandwiches, ploughman's lunches and salads on the menu. Hot daily specials listed on a blackboard may include spicy minestrone soup, liver, bacon and onion, and game pie. Regular monthly Austrian speciality evenings are a great attraction. Food is served from 12 noon to 2 pm and 7 pm to 10 pm (Sunday 9 pm).

To the rear of the inn there is a large lawned garden with picnic benches and children's play equipment. Children are also welcome indoors, where they have their own menu to choose from, and dogs are allowed in if on leads. The pub is open from 11 am to 3 pm and 7 pm to 11 pm (Sunday 12 noon to 3 pm and 7 pm to 10.30 pm).

Telephone: 01303 813334.

How to get there: Brabourne is situated beyond Brabourne Lees, 2½ miles north-east of the A20 Ashford to Folkestone road, 5½ miles east of Ashford. The village lies north of the M20, midway between junctions 10 and 11.

Parking: The inn has its own car park.

Length of the walk: 3 miles. Map: OS Landranger 179 Canterbury and East Kent or 189 Ashford and Romney Marsh (inn GR 100419).

When you have strolled along the village street and explored the fascinating parish church and its treasures, this delightful short ramble traverses farmland paths before ascending the Pilgrims' Way and the well-waymarked North Downs Way to reach the crest of the Downs and wonderful panoramic views. Some of the field paths can be muddy, especially after rain or ploughing, otherwise, the route follows good tracks and short stretches of quiet metalled lanes. One steady climb up the scarp face of the Downs.

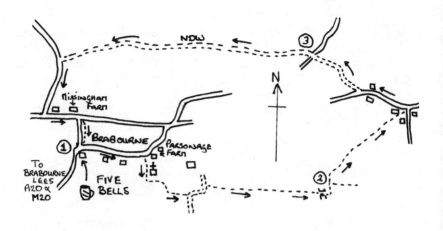

The Walk

1 On leaving the pub turn right along the village street, then as the lane bears left in front of Parsonage Farm, take the arrowed footpath right into the churchyard. The unusual and ancient flint-walled church of St Mary the Virgin is well worth closer inspection, as it features a wide, heavily buttressed 12th-century tower and, more notably, a fine Norman chancel. Here, you will find intricately carved capitals, an original, and probably unique, 12th-century stained-glass window, a very rare heart-shrine of Balliol College's founder – John de Baliol – who died in 1269, a Bethersden marble tomb-chest and splendid intact floor brasses to the local Scot family. Also of note are the Scot chapel and the 30 ft medieval ladder leading to the belfry. The informative church guide will enhance your tour of the church.

Follow the path to the right of the church to a gate, then turn left (blue arrow) and walk around the field edge, soon to cross a wooden footbridge to join a farm track. Keep left, then just beyond a sharp left bend, turn right with the waymarker post to follow a defined path across a large open field between crops. On reaching the perimeter of the field go through a line of trees, crossing a footbridge over a stream and a stile into a further field. Turn left to a stile in the field corner.

2 Follow the direction of the blue arrow on the stile, bearing slightly right uphill (this may not be clearly defined) across a large field, soon to spot a stile ahead leading into an adjacent field. Head diagonally right across the field towards farm buildings, eventually reaching a junction of lanes by a telephone box on the edge of

Stowting. Turn left, then immediately left again at the junction and shortly begin to ascend the quiet lane (Pilgrims' Way). As it levels out, take the waymarked byway on your right (North Downs Way), an ancient and stony hedged track that climbs steadily to the top of the North Downs. Just before reaching a lane, pause to catch your breath at the superbly positioned bench on your left, which affords out-standing far-reaching views across the Weald.

3 Cross the lane and continue along the North Downs Way, this time maintaining the magnificent rural views, as you make your way north-westwards along the ridge. In ½ mile reach another lane and turn left, heading downhill to a T-junction with the Pilgrims' Way. Follow it left and pass Missingham Farm, then just beyond the road junction on your right, climb the stile in the hedge into an orchard. Walk along the right-hand edge of the orchard to a stile beyond a line of tall fir trees and cross the village lane back into the pub car park.

Places of interest nearby

At Brook (3 miles north-west) is the *Wye College Agricultural Museum* which houses a comprehensive collection of farm imple-ments and tools in a preserved late 14th-century barn and early 19th-century oast house. Telephone: 01233 812401. Just south of Mersham (5 miles south-west) is *Swanton Mill*, a weatherboarded watermill in full working order and grinding wholemeal flour which is for sale. Milling museum and extensive gardens. Open weekend afternoons in summer. Further exploration will reveal *Port Lympne Wild Animal Park, Mansion and Gardens* (5 miles south) with its rare and endangered species, safari trail and Dutch colonial-style mansion. Open daily. Telephone: 01303 264646. A mile from the animal park is *Lympne Castle,* built in 1360, with a Great Hall flanked by Norman and medieval towers and affording superb views across the Romney Marsh. Open Easter to September. Telephone: 01303 267571.

16 Pett Bottom
The Duck Inn

Enjoying a very tranquil setting in a charming valley and looking out over rolling countryside, the attractive tile-hung Duck Inn dates from 1621 when it was built as a shepherd's cottage for the local estate. It became an alehouse and grocer's shop serving the local farming community in 1849 and was only granted a full licence in 1904, when it was called the Woodmans Arms. The pub acquired its present name in the 1960s. Ian Fleming, the creator of the James Bond books, used to live nearby and was a regular customer, presumably ordering dry martinis, shaken but not stirred! Fleming featured the pub in his Bond novel, *Moonraker*.

The Duck is a favoured country destination locally for a relaxing drink or meal in delightfully traditional surroundings. The classic, unspoilt interior comprises two cosy bars and an adjacent restaurant, all, thankfully, devoid of intrusive piped music and electronic games. The separate, tiny snug bar – 007 Bar – has a rustic charm with stripped pine floorboards, tongue and groove walls and ceiling, a large scrubbed pine table and various pews and a few mahogany tables and chairs. The carpeted lounge bar boasts stripped tables, a good winter log fire in a fine 17th-century fireplace, a hop adorned ceiling and unusual hessian curtains, while fresh flowers and candles enhance the dining ambience in the connecting restaurant.

The pub is a welcoming freehouse dispensing Burton Bridge Bitter, Greene King Abbot Ale – 'Rabbits Tail' to the initiated – and a seasonal Greene King brew, such as Black Baron, straight from the cask. Theobalds cider, a deceptively strong local scrumpy, occasionally makes an appearance behind the bar. This rural hideaway draws a loyal dining clientele from far and wide, as the blackboard menu lists an interesting and varied choice of home-cooked meals. Hearty snacks or starters may include country vegetable soup, garlic fish pâté, salad Niçoise and cheese and pasta salad, with main courses like beef lasagne, spicy beef stew and dumplings, chilli con carne and popular, generously filled home-made pies – steak and oyster, pig and claret, lamb, apricot and ginger and beef and Guinness. Vegetarians are spoilt for choice with cauliflower cheese, vegetable curry and vegetable, basil and tomato pie among the dishes available. Hot chocolate fudge cake and orange and ginger pudding appear on the pudding list. A three-course lunch is available on Sunday. Imaginative evening restaurant fare is chalked up on a separate blackboard menu. Food is available from 12 noon to 2.15 pm and 6.30 pm to 9.45 pm (Sunday and Monday 9 pm).

Peaceful summer al fresco drinking can be enjoyed in the sheltered side garden, or at one of the front picnic benches with views across open fields. Children are allowed in the snug bar and dogs are made very welcome. The bar is open from 11.30 am to 3 pm and 6.30 pm to 11 pm (Sunday 12 noon to 4 pm and 7 pm to 10.30 pm).

Telephone: 01227 830354.

How to get there: The isolated hamlet of Pett Bottom is situated on a rural lane 2½ miles south-west of Bridge, which lies off the A2 and A2050 some 3 miles south-east of Canterbury. It is well signposted and can also be reached from the B2068 Canterbury to Hythe road, via Lower Hardres.

Parking: There is adequate car parking to the side of the pub.

Length of the walk: 3¼ miles. Map: OS Landranger 179 Canterbury and East Kent or 189 Ashford and Romney Marsh (inn GR 161520).

A varied and easy short walk along a delightful mixture of scenic farmland paths and woodland bridleways through peaceful, rolling downland south of Canterbury. It incorporates the straggling village of Lower Hardres with its 19th-century church and tales of the old East Kent custom of hoodening. Generally well waymarked and firm underfoot.

The Walk

1 From the pub turn right along the lane and take the first turning left to pass a farm. Climb uphill along a narrow lane, soon to keep right at a fork and continue to gently ascend. At a hedge on your left, cross a hidden stile and proceed along the left-hand edge of a field, shortly to follow the established path across the field – good valley views – to reach a stile in the field corner by woodland. Bear left along the edge of Stockfield Wood, eventually reaching a lane beside the 18th-century Three Horseshoes pub in Lower Hardres.

Cross the village road into a narrow lane, signposted 'Catt' and 'Stone Street'. Follow this wooded lane, then in 200 yards take the arrowed bridleway right which passes through a wide grassy swathe between woods. Descend into the shallow valley bottom, then as the track bears left, veer off right through trees to reach a green metal gate. Head across the centre of a field through the base of the valley and, shortly, pass through a farm with a farm shop to follow the metalled driveway to a road.

2 Cross straight over into Church Lane, signposted 'Pett Bottom', and soon reach the parish church. Built in about 1820 on the site of a 13th-century church, it has often been described as 'ugly' but its interior is Early English in style and it possesses a lofty octagonal steeple and spire. The churchyard is a delight in early spring when it is carpeted with snowdrops. Lower Hardres is also noted for a curious story concerning the old Kent custom of hoodening, in which a crudely carved wooden horse's head on a stick is carried by a man from house to house in a jovial or frolicking manner, collecting money or food for a Christmas feast. The story states that in 1859 hoodeners visited the Rectory, where an invalid German lady who had not walked for seven years was staying. One particular per-forming hoodener pretended to jump at her with vicious jaws snapping close to her face, which frightened her so much that she leapt out of her chair and ran into the house. The tale ends with the wooden horse being bought and taken back to Germany.

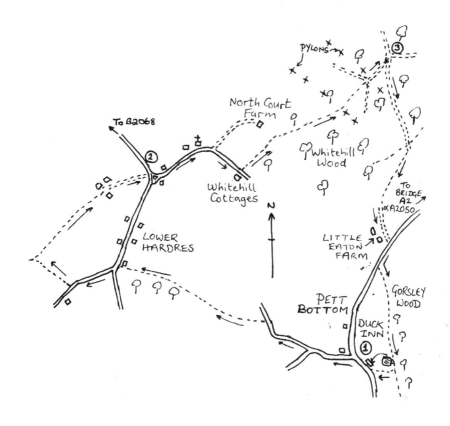

Beyond the church bear right at a fork towards Whitehill Cottages, opposite which you turn left with the concrete bridleway sign to join a splendid path through Whitehill Wood, a beautiful chestnut, coppiced woodland. Keep to the main path for ½ mile, disregarding any tracks branching off, to emerge out into a clearing. Pass beneath the first set of power lines, then at a junction of several tracks, keep straight on to pass under the second set of power lines, with a pheasant enclosure away to your left.

3 Shortly, at a crossing of paths (waymarker post), turn sharp right onto a grassy path (it looks as though you are doubling back), which soon curves left along the edge of a clearing. On reaching an arrowed post continue ahead, then at a second post near a fork of paths, follow the blue arrow left and descend on an excellent path along the woodland fringe. Eventually reach a gate, enter pasture and walk along a line of oak trees, then at a marker post proceed across the field to a metal gate.

Follow a fenced path and soon pass Little Eaton Farm to reach a lane. Turn right and in 100 yards cross the waymarked stile on your left. Bear diagonally right uphill on a defined path, then at a grassy track, briefly turn left and pick up the diagonal path again across the field to a stile on the edge of woodland. Proceed through the edge of Gorsley Wood, then at an arrowed post turn right through scrub and downhill on a worn path across a field to the lane beside the Duck Inn.

Places of interest nearby

Near Littlebourne (4 miles north-east) is *Howletts Wildlife Park* which houses the world's largest collection of gorillas and tigers, as well as other interesting animals. Cafeteria and picnic sites. Open daily. Telephone: 01227 721286. *Stelling Minnis Windmill* (4 miles south) is a black smock mill built in 1886 and recently restored, with a 1912 oil engine powering the mill for grinding demonstrations. Open on summer Sundays. At Barham (south-east) *Elham Valley Vineyards* are open to the public, offering self-guided tours and wine tastings. Telephone: 01227 831266. The cathedral city of *Canterbury* has a wealth of historic buildings and fascinating museums to explore.

Bridge ✓
The White Horse Inn

Since being bypassed in the mid-1970s, the straggling village of Bridge is now, thankfully, a peaceful backwater away from the heavy lorries, noise and fumes of the busy A2 Dover road. However, long before being disturbed by modern-day traffic, the village was a popular stopping-off point for travellers using the old London to Dover coaching road. The destination for both weary horses and passengers was the attractive 16th-century White Horse Inn, which enjoys a central position on the main street of the village. The inn was known as a baiting or halting-house, as the village was not really far enough from Dover to be classed as a full stage but it was, however, a convenient stopping place for a change of horses and much needed refreshment. The main bar of the inn is thought to have been a blacksmith's forge during this era, servicing the needs of the hard-working horses.

The spick and span and well-appointed interior of the inn comprises three character bars and a comfortable restaurant. The main bar boasts plenty of beams, half-panelled oak walls, a wealth of gleaming brass and copper artefacts and an enormous fireplace with a huge carved lintel featuring an inscription, which is thought to have Civil War connections. Other areas are tastefully furnished with pine tables and colourful fabrics, and adorned with various old hunting prints and firearms. A welcoming and cosy dining atmosphere prevails in this well-run establishment. Upstairs, there is one en suite letting bedroom.

The inn is part of the Pubmaster chain of pubs and dispenses a good range of drinks from its well-stocked bar. Among the real ales on handpump are Bass, Flowers Original, Boddingtons and Whitbread Castle Eden Ale, as well as draught Addlestones cider, over 35 malt whiskies and an interesting selection of global wines, including good value wines of the month and a few Kentish wines. A varied and extensive menu offers an excellent choice of ploughman's lunches and freshly-cut sandwiches, starters and light meals, like home-made soup, pan-fried sardines with garlic and seafood crêpes, and regular home-cooked main meals, such as grilled liver and bacon, pan-fried sirloin steak in red wine and black peppercorn sauce and grilled trout with prawns and mushrooms. A large blackboard menu lists the range of daily specials available, which may include tomato, feta cheese and olive salad, steak and kidney pudding, rack of lamb and fish dishes like medallions of monkfish in tarragon and white wine, or grilled whole plaice. Also of interest at this popular food establishment are the summer Sunday lunchtime barbecues, winter three-course Sunday lunches and the occasional Indian, buffet-style, curry nights. Food is served daily from 12 noon to 2 pm and 6.30 pm (7 pm Sunday) to 9.30 pm.

To the rear of the inn is a good lawned garden with picnic benches, and children and dogs are welcome inside. The bar is open from 11 am to 3 pm and 6 pm to 11 pm (Sunday 12 noon to 3 pm and 7 pm to 10.30 pm).

Telephone: 01227 830249.

How to get there: Bridge is located ½ mile off the A2 Canterbury to Dover road, 3 miles south-east of Canterbury. The inn will be found in the centre of the High Street.

Parking: The inn has its own car park. Alternatively, park at the recreation ground along Patrixbourne Road, or along the High Street.

Length of the walk: 3 miles. Map: OS Landranger 179 Canterbury and East Kent or 189 Ashford and Romney Marsh (inn GR 183545).

This peaceful stroll explores part of the delightful valley of the Nail Bourne, one of Kent's numerous 'intermittent' streams, which vanishes and reappears as it flows for 15 attractive miles through gently undulating downland countryside and several charming villages. Field paths and farm tracks lead to idyllic Bishopsbourne with its fascinating church and literary connections, returning to Bridge via the Elham Valley Way, which traverses beautiful Bourne Park. Few hills and generally firm underfoot, except near the river in winter.

The Walk

1 On leaving the White Horse turn left along the High Street and, shortly, turn right beside the 300 year old Plough and Harrow (formerly a maltings and brewery) into Brewery Lane. Beyond a sharp right-hand bend, take the waymarked footpath (fingerpost) on your left and proceed through pasture, soon to cross two footbridges over the lazily flowing Nail Bourne stream, then bear left to a kissing-gate. During very dry summers this tiny river may stop flowing altogether but occasionally, especially after prolonged wet periods, the stream rises suddenly, flooding adjacent land.

Immediately beyond the kissing-gate, at a choice of waymarked paths, keep left, parallel with the stream, with the tall and impressive Dutch, brick-built Bridge Place beyond the wall on your left. In a short distance, bear off slightly right on a worn path to reach a stile and a metalled track. Turn right, soon to follow the track left as the tarmac gives way to a rough track in front of Flint Cottage. Continue beside hop fields and maintain direction on this good track to the rear of Bourne Park and House, eventually reaching Lenhall Farm.

2 Just before a large oast-topped farm building, turn left and follow the metalled access drive out to a lane. Keep left along the lane, soon to cross the bridge over the disused Elham Valley railway line (the refurbished old station is visible on the left) to enter Bishopsbourne. Climb the arrowed stile on your right and head across pasture towards a telegraph pole, crossing a waymarked stile beside a tree. Turn left downhill along a hedged path into the village, merging with Park Lane to reach the main village street beside the Mermaid Inn and Old Post Office.

Turn left along the pretty, cottage-lined street and pass the Old

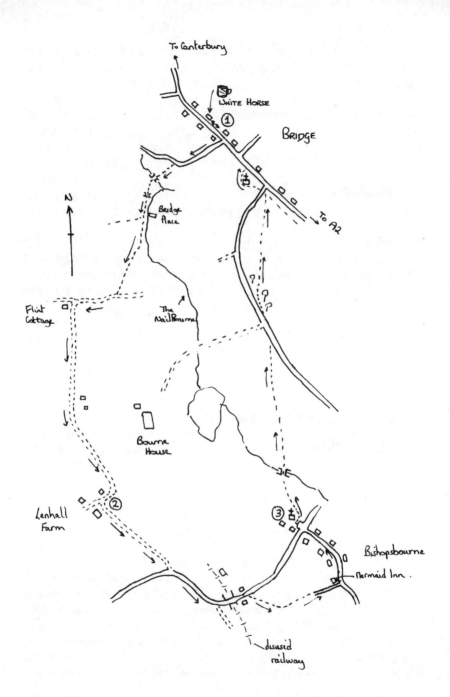

To Canterbury

WHITE HORSE

① BRIDGE

To A2

N

Bridge Place

Flint Cottage

The Nailbourne

Bourne House

Lenhall Farm

②

③

Bishopsbourne

Mermaid Inn.

disused railway

Forge and a plaque informing you that the author and poet Jocelyn Brook, who wrote an authorative book on orchids, used to live in the village, then continue to a T-junction, opposite a giant horse chestnut tree, war memorial and the parish church. The village links with the literary world extend to the Polish-born novelist Joseph Conrad, who lived and wrote in the house known as Oswalds, the former rectory located adjacent to the church, during the 1920s. Cross the road, enter the churchyard and take time to look round the 13th-century church of St Mary, noting the fine stained-glass windows, some dating from the 14th century, but especially the delicate Burne-Jones window in the tower, with colourful pre-Raphaelite figures and fruit trees.

3   Bear immediately right with the arrow on entering the churchyard and follow the path round its perimeter to climb a stile into open parkland – Bourne Park. Proceed ahead with the waymarker arrow, pausing to view the attractive scene of church and neighbouring Court Lodge behind you. Cross a bridge over the course of the Nail Bourne and follow the well-waymarked route across the splendid, sheep-grazed park, with the magnificent Queen Anne mansion (not open) and lake visible to your left. Climb a stile and continue the diagonal route through pasture to a further stile and lane. Turn left along the lane, pass the driveway to Bourne Park and, shortly, bear off right with the fingerpost (Elham Valley Way) and gently ascend a path through Warren Plantation to a stile.

Bear diagonally left across pasture (yellow arrows on posts), with delightful views towards Bridge Place and across the valley, eventually reaching a stile in the field corner and the edge of Bridge village. Cross the lane into St Peter's churchyard, following the tarmac path to the village High Street and turn left for the inn.

Places of interest nearby

Beyond the picturesque villages of Patrixbourne and Bekesbourne is *Howletts Wildlife Park* (2 miles north-east) which houses, among other animals, the world's largest collection of gorillas and tigers. Telephone: 01227 721286. Nestling on the river Stour, north-east of historic Canterbury, is charming *Fordwich* with its timber-framed Tudor town hall and courtroom, thought to be the oldest and smallest in England. Telephone: 01227 710610. Bird-watchers will find *Stodmarsh Nature Reserve* (5½ miles north-east) a superb wetland area for a wide variety of species.

18 Chillenden ✓
The Griffin's Head

Tucked away in a tiny farming hamlet amid rolling open countryside, the Griffin's Head is an architectural gem of a building that oozes charm and character throughout. Dating from 1286, it is a fine black and white half-timbered Wealden hall house, and was originally built as a farmhouse to serve the estate of John de Chillenden. During the reign of Henry IV it became the property of the church and was used to house monks, who also farmed the adjacent land, until the Dissolution of the Monasteries in 1539. It reverted back to being a farm and, like many estate farms, began to brew ale and cider for the local community, being given an ale licence in 1743 so that the rector could hold tithe suppers in the building. It was not until 1766, through the popularity of the then main Canterbury to Deal coaching road, that a full licence was granted and the present name acquired. The Griffin – a mythical half-bird/half-lion creature – was derived from the coat of arms of the D'Aeth family, who were lords of the manor for several generations.

The present Tudor timbered structure is built around the original wattle and daub walls, some of which can be seen in the splendid interior. Three delightfully unspoilt rooms feature flagstone floors, exposed brick walls and beams, an enormous inglenook with a warming log fire on cold days and a tasteful mix of furnishings, from old scrubbed pine tables and chairs to church pews. Walls are adorned with various prints and wooden wine box ends, and there is also a small collection of old oil lamps.

Shepherd Neame own this magnificent pub which dispenses their Master Brew, Best Bitter, Spitfire, Bishops Finger and Porter (winter) real ales on handpump. Wine drinkers can choose from an above average list of global wines, including some interesting bin ends and often a good value wine of the week. A twice-daily changing menu, listed on a blackboard above the fire, highlights the short and varied range of dishes on offer. Lighter bites include ploughman's lunches, a home-made pâté and freshly-made soup, such as thick vegetable, or tomato and feta cheese salad, grilled smoked sprats and seafood Mornay. Heartier meals may feature cottage pie, lambs' liver and bacon, bubble and squeak with ham, lamb and Stilton pie and chicken breast stuffed with cream cheese, mushroom and bacon. Evening extras include a few fresh fish dishes – sea bass and salmon for example. Finish off with a home-made pudding, like apple and toffee crumble, tiramisu and lemon and almond Bakewell tart. Summer al fresco barbecues are a popular attraction. Food is served daily from 12 noon to 2 pm and 7 pm to 9.30 pm.

Fine weather drinking can be enjoyed in the attractive rose-filled garden. Dogs (on leads) and well-behaved children are welcome inside. The Griffin is open from 11 am to 11 pm on Monday to Saturday and from 12 noon to 3 pm and 7 pm to 10.30 pm on Sunday.

Telephone: 01304 840325.

How to get there: Chillenden is located south of the A257 Canterbury to Sandwich road and is signposted 2½ miles off the B2046, just south of Wingham. The village is also easily reached from the A256 Sandwich to Dover road, turning off near Betteshanger. The pub is situated on the south-eastern edge of the village beyond the church.

Parking: The inn has its own car park. Alternatively, there is a small parking area along the lane near the telephone box.

Length of the walk: 3½ miles. Map: OS Landranger 179 Canterbury and East Kent (inn GR 271536).

After a stroll through the village, with the option of a short diversion to visit Chillenden Windmill, this interesting walk traverses farmland paths to the unspoilt estate village of Goodnestone, complete with fine manor house and 14 acre garden (open) set in attractive parkland. Return via the park and scenic field paths and bridleways back to Chillenden. Few hills and easy going underfoot.

The Walk

1 On leaving the pub turn right along the village lane and pass some fine timbered farmhouses and the tiny grey flint church of All Saints, which retains a good many Norman features. Go round a sharp right-hand bend beyond Chillenden Court Farm and then take the arrowed footpath on your left, beside a quaint thatched cottage. However, if you wish to visit Chillenden's fine windmill, keep ahead along the lane for ¼ mile. Constructed in 1868 and restored in 1958, this open trestle post mill was one of the last of its type to be built in the county and stands on an exposed site above the village. To continue the walk, return to the footpath, then cross a track and head towards the fingerpost visible ahead, cutting across the corner of a field to a lane.

Cross over and ascend a narrow path through scrub into an arable field. Keep to the left-hand edge, parallel with the road, then at the field edge turn right alongside the fence, soon to climb a stile on your left. Proceed straight across a large open field on a defined path to a further stile and a lane. Negotiate the stile opposite and enter Long Wood, a fine oak and beech woodland. Shortly, cross an earth track and follow the clear path close to the woodland edge to reach a stile, then bear diagonally right on a worn field path towards Goodnestone and enter the village playing field. Keep left to join a concrete track leading to the village lane.

2 This classic estate village has a timeless atmosphere. Having explored a little, follow the lane towards Goodnestone Park and the fine 18th-century house. Jane Austen was a frequent visitor here as her brother Edward married one of the Brook-Bridges daughters and she mentions the house and village in her letters. The house is surrounded by a 14 acre garden with terraced lawns, small arboretum and walled garden.

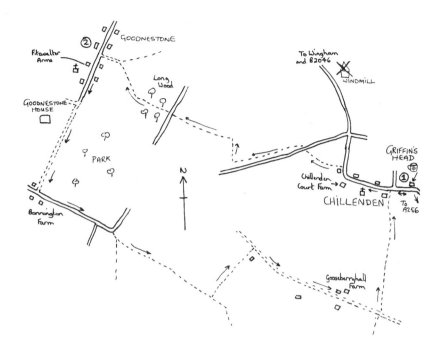

Pass the car park and entrance to Goodnestone Park Gardens and walk to the side of a white gate to follow a 'private road' across the park, in front of the wall to the main house, eventually reaching a lane opposite a splendid timbered building. Turn left, pass Bonnington Farm, then on reaching a sharp left-hand bend, bear off right along an arrowed footpath. Almost immediately, keep left at a fork of paths and follow a defined track through the centre of a field, along a line of telegraph poles. Climb a stile in the field corner, proceed along the right-hand edge of the next field and keep to the path into the following field of rough grassland. Turn immediately left along a narrow, worn path to an arrowed gate beside a water tank.

Follow the right-hand edge of the field, soon to pass an isolated cottage to join a grass-centred track (Cherrygarden Lane). Turn right and gently descend, passing through a small wood and beside Gooseberryhall Farm, then just beyond a paddock, turn left along a bridleway (blue arrow). Follow this back into Chillenden, turning right by Yew Tree Farm along the village street back to the Griffin's Head.

Alkham ✓
The Marquis of Granby

Alkham is an attractive little village that nestles among the woods and chalk hills in the deep Alkham valley, a short drive from the coast and Dover. A number of historic buildings, including several medieval hall houses and the handsome 18th-century Old Rectory, cluster around the oldest building in the village, the early 13th-century flint and ragstone church, which was built by monks of nearby St Radigund's Abbey. Its interior boasts the tomb of the first known rector, Herbert de Averanches 1199-1203, and the inscription is thought to be the oldest in any Kent church.

At the bottom of the lane from the church stands the rather more recent (1810) Marquis of Granby pub, which replaced the Prince of Orange alehouse (1770) that once occupied one of the cottages between the present pub and the churchyard. Set above the road overlooking the village and green, the white-painted Marquis of Granby was, at one time, the real hub of the community. Part of the premises was a shop selling animal feed to the villagers and auctions of wood and properties were once conducted here. Today, it is a homely and unpretentious village local, its single open-plan bar featuring two open fireplaces, simple darkwood tables and chairs, comfortable cushioned wall bench seating and several photographs of the village in bygone days adorning the walls. There is also a separate restaurant.

The pub is a very welcoming freehouse serving a good range of real ales – Young's Special, Fuller's London Pride, Shepherd Neame Master Brew and Ruddles County – on handpump. An extensive blackboard menu lists a varied range of dishes to suit all tastes and appetites. Those popping in for just a snack can choose from salads, ploughman's lunches, filled jacket potatoes – coronation chicken, prawn surprise – filled baguettes and pizzas. Generous main meals include moussaka, steak and ale pie, chicken, ham and mushroom pie and several Indian dishes, like chicken tikka masala and lamb rogan josh. However, the speciality here is the excellent choice of fresh fish available from Wednesday to Saturday. The separate board may highlight French fish soup, whole lobster, wild Scottish oak smoked salmon, Dover sole, whole sea bass poached in white wine with ginger and dill and the very popular freshly-battered cod and chips. Vegetarians are looked after well and those with room to spare can tuck into spotted dick or treacle sponge for pudding. There is a traditional roast lunch on a Sunday. Food is served from 11 am to 2 pm and 6 pm to 9.30 pm (Sunday 12 noon to 2 pm and 7 pm to 9.30 pm).

To the rear of the pub is a lawned garden with mature trees and picnic benches – ideal for fine weather drinking. Children, but not dogs, are welcome indoors. The bar is open from 11 am to 3 pm and 6 pm to 11 pm (Sunday 12 noon to 3 pm and 7 pm to 10.30 pm).

Telephone: 01304 822945.

How to get there: Alkham is situated midway along the Alkham Valley Road (the B2060) between Temple Ewell (just off the A256, 2 miles north of Dover) and the A260 near Hawkinge (1½ miles north of Folkestone and 2 miles from junction 13 of the M20). The pub is located in the centre of the village.

Parking: The pub has its own car park. Alternatively, park beside the village green.

Length of the walk: 4 miles. Map: OS Landranger 179 Canterbury and East Kent (inn GR 256423).

An undulating walk that dips and climbs through the picturesque Alkham valley via well-waymarked footpaths and bridleways. Of interest along the way are the pretty village of Alkham itself, the ruins of 12th-century St Radigund's Abbey and delightful chalk valley views. One or two steep climbs but generally easy going underfoot.

The Walk

1 From the pub turn left along the village road – can be fast and busy – then at the green take the waymarked footpath right across its centre. Pass the cricket pavilion and on reaching the course of the intermittently flowing Alkham or Drellingore Nailbourne, which has been known to flood part of the green to create a pond, bear left to cross a footbridge in the corner of the green. Follow the path left between fencing and fir trees, soon to emerge onto a pitted driveway beside houses. Almost immediately, look out for an unsigned narrow path between panelled fencing on your right, which gently ascends to a stile and farm track.

Cross the track and stile opposite and bear half-left uphill across pasture to a further stile, with splendid views unfolding behind you across the village. Ascend steadily in the same direction, via two more stiles, then keep right-handed alongside woodland to a gate in the field corner. Climb into the wood, then at a T-junction with a bridleway, turn left uphill through attractive mixed woodland. The path soon levels out to reach a lane beside a house called Mount Ararat.

2 Turn left along the quiet lane, then shortly cross an arrowed stile on your right and head diagonally left across a large open field, towards a stile located beside a dead tree. Beyond a small footbridge, head straight across the next field (not signed) to reach a concrete drive/way and the extensive ruins of St Radigund's Abbey. The abbey was founded in 1192 and was built on a fairly large scale, but since 1590 it has been used as a farm. The creeper-covered gatehouse used to be the tower of the church and the attractive Elizabethan farmhouse was created from the refectory.

Turn left along the drive to a road junction and cross straight over, signed 'River'. In a short distance, turn left by a broken concrete footpath marker onto a grass-centred track. Pass the entrance to an old yard and follow the path as it bears right along the fringe of woodland. When you are parallel to a farm building on your right, head into and descend through Stonyhill Wood on a good path to a gate.

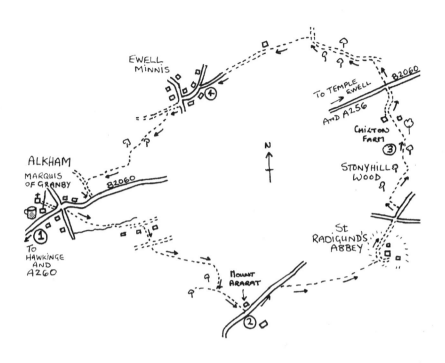

3 Continue downhill along the right-hand edge of a field, go through an arrowed gate and descend to Chilton Farm, following the farm drive out to the Alkham Valley Road. Cross straight over – taking great care – to join a bridleway that crosses MOD land. Initially, ascend steadily along a hedged track, then merge with a wide stony track and bear left to steeply climb up the valley side with superb views through the Alkham valley. Continue climbing through woodland, eventually reaching a cattle-grid and junction of paths. Do not cross the grid. Instead, turn left along a hedged bridleway which becomes metalled after 300 yards, then pass Sunnyhill Farm and continue into Ewell Minnis.

4 At a T-junction bear left, then by the telephone box in the village centre, turn left, then right onto a waymarked bridleway. In a few yards go through a swing gate on your left and bear diagonally right with the fingerpost across pasture, shortly descending to a wooden swing gate and entering Sladden Wood Nature Reserve. This ancient coppiced woodland is home to a diverse range of plants, notably rare herb paris, green hellebore and lady orchid. Leave the reserve by a

Slip Lane, Alkham.

further gate, then bear half-right to skirt round the base of a steep hill (farm ahead in the valley) and keep right to reach a gate in the field corner. Pass behind dwellings and gardens, keep right at a fork of paths and soon reach a tarmac lane. Turn left downhill to the main village road, following it right by the green back to the pub.

Places of interest nearby

The attractions of both *Dover* and *Folkestone* are only a few miles away, as are *MacFarlanes Butterfly Farm* (telephone: 01303 844244) at Swingfield (4½ miles west), the *Kent Battle of Britain Museum* (telephone: 01303 893140) at Hawkinge (5 miles west) displaying the world's largest collection of recovered remains of RAF and Luftwaffe aircraft, as well as vehicles and weapons, and the *Eurotunnel Exhibition Centre* (telephone: 01303 270111) at Cheriton, near Folkestone (7 miles south-west). *Crabble Corn Mill* (2½ miles east at River, near Dover) is a beautiful Georgian watermill with lakeside café, children's activities and arts and crafts. Telephone: 01304 823292.

20 West Hougham ✓
The Chequers

Occupying a lofty downland position between Dover and Folkestone, and only 1½ miles from the coast and towering chalk cliffs, West Hougham is an isolated rural community comprising a pleasant mix of old and new dwellings. Probably one of the oldest buildings in the village, although much modernised in recent years, is the salmon pink-washed and timbered Chequers pub which reputedly dates back to 1507 and the reign of Henry VII. Originally a yeoman's house with adjoining barn, stables and 2½ acres of land, it presumably brewed ale for the village before obtaining its licence and present name in 1703. The Chequers continued to keep cows on its smallholding, as well as functioning as an inn, until 1926 when Fremlins Brewery acquired the premises. Today the pub is a popular and friendly freehouse.

The original small cottage has been extended to provide a spacious open-plan interior, featuring a central fireplace with gas 'log-effect' fire, low old and new ceiling beams, mainly darkwood and pine furniture, part modern flagstone and part carpeted floors and an interesting collection of bygones and farming memorabilia adorning the walls, or hanging from the ceiling. A section of the room houses a pool table and the neat dining area leads to the attractive rear terrace, complete with a loggia bedecked with climbing clematis.

There is one real ale – John Smith's Bitter – on handpump, which accompanies Foster's and Kronenbourg 1664 lager and Beamish stout. Bar food ranges from standard pub favourites like prawn cocktail, garlic bread, breaded cod, scampi and chips and sirloin steak to fresh trout, various omelettes, sweet and sour pork and a choice of curries. Ploughman's lunches, but not sandwiches, are readily available. The attraction on Monday and Tuesday lunchtimes is the excellent roast dinner and sweet – fresh fruit sundae or steamed chocolate pudding – available at an unbelievable inclusive price. Food is served every day from 12 noon to 2 pm and 7 pm to 9.30 pm.

Dogs are welcome inside but children under 8 are not allowed indoors. The bar is open from 12 noon to 3 pm and 7 pm to 11 pm (10.30 pm on Sunday).

Telephone: 01304 201907.

How to get there: West Hougham lies 1½ miles north of the B2011 between Dover and Folkestone, 3½ miles west of Dover and 1½ miles north-east of the A20. The Chequers is located along The Street in the centre of the village, near the post office and stores.

Parking: The pub has a car park to the front and there is limited space along The Street.

Length of the walk: 3¼ miles. Map: OS Landranger 179 Canterbury and East Kent (inn GR 266403).

An enjoyable rural ramble across open downland and through a dry chalk valley, via good and generally well-waymarked bridle-ways and field paths, affording splendid views towards Dover Castle and out to sea. Take time to obtain the key and view the tiny and remote Capel-le-Ferne church.

The Walk

1 Leave the pub and turn right along The Street, then just beyond the left turning for Alkham and River, take the waymarked bridleway along a wide stony track and pass a few houses. Your route soon

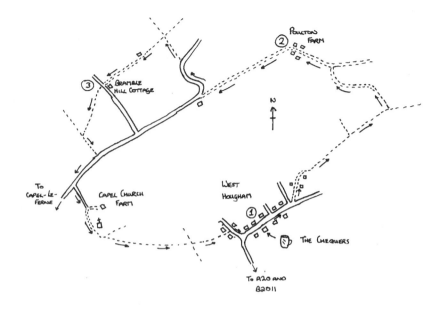

narrows to a well-defined bridleway between open fields and shortly affords some fine views across Dover, with the massive Norman keep of Dover Castle dominating the scene. Pass beneath some power lines and, in a few yards, go through a heavily-weighted gate on your left (unsigned). Head straight across pasture towards a tree with scramble-bike tracks etched on the hillside beyond. Begin to descend and pass through a gate to join a rough track, noting the blue arrowed post, and proceed steadily downhill into the dry valley bottom. Reach a metalled track, opposite an old and, unfortunately, rather neglected area once used for scramble-bike racing, and turn left along the track towards farm buildings (Poulton Farm).

2   Continue through the farmyard, emerging onto a stony track that gently ascends through the valley to a lane. Turn right and steeply climb uphill, then at a sharp right-hand bend, negotiate the stile on your left. Go straight across the field, bearing slightly left to cross a stile in the perimeter fence and turn left at a crossing of routes along a narrow, fenced path. Shortly, pass in front of an isolated house and merge with its metalled drive, following it to a lane beside Bramble Hill Cottage.

3   Proceed straight across to climb a waymarked stile and then bear half-left through an open crop field, aiming towards the pylon, to join a wide grassy bridleway on the field edge. Keep left and eventually reach a gate and lane. Turn right, then in 200 yards turn left along a tarmac drive to Capel Church Farm, signposted 'Church of St Mary the Virgin'. On nearing the farm, keep right with the sign for the church (key available from the farm) and soon reach the lychgate to this peacefully positioned redundant building. If you do have time to explore inside, note the rare stone – not the usual wooden – rood screen across the chancel with three simple pointed arches. The churchyard is a delight, often sheep-grazed, and colourful in spring.

Leave the lychgate and continue left into the field. Walk alongside the churchyard wall, then at a telegraph pole (overgrown stile and yellow arrow) turn left. Almost immediately, bear diagonally right across the field, following the line of telegraph poles to a stile in a hedgerow. Head straight over the next field, pass through a wide gap in the hedge and proceed on a worn path across a third field towards houses, Climb a stile and walk along a narrow, fenced path to a lane, where you turn right, then left by West Hougham village hall into The Street for the short stroll back to the pub.

Places of interest nearby

The ferry port town of *Dover* (3½ miles east) offers a wealth of attractions, including its impressive *Castle* (Norman keep, Saxon church and Hellfire Corner exhibition, telephone: 01304 201628), the award-winning *White Cliffs Experience* which explains 2,000 years of Dover's history through audio-visual and visual shows (telephone: 01304 210101), *Dover Old Town Gaol* in which you take a journey back in time to Victorian England and experience the horrors of life behind bars (telephone: 01304 242766) and *Dover Transport Museum* which houses a varied collection of road vehicles (telephone: 01304 204612). At *Folkestone Warren* (2 miles south-west) are some 350 acres of natural coastal habitat with overgrown scrub. The chalk cliffs here are of interest for rock structure, plant, insects and birdlife – a network of footpaths and a visitor centre with natural history displays in a martello tower (telephone: 01303 258594). The *Kent Battle of Britain Museum* at Hawkinge (5 miles west) is home to the largest collection of authentic relics and related memorabilia of British and German aircraft involved in the fighting, including full-size replicas of the Hurricane, Spitfire and Me-109 (telephone: 01303 893140).